EXTRACTING THE GOOD: THE IMPORTANCE OF SELF-LOVE

By

ALBERTA LAMPKINS

COPYRIGHTS

Copyright © 2023 by Alberta Lampkins:

All rights reserved. This book or any portion thereof may not be reproduced or used in any manner without the author's express written permission except for brief quotations in a book review.

Published by A.L. Savvy Publications. For information, address alsavvypublications@gmail.com.

July 2023
First Edition
ISBN: 978-0-9903805-8-0

Praise for *Extracting the Good: The Importance of Self-Love*

"Alberta Lampkins has done it again with her latest literary work, *Extracting the Good: The Importance of Self-Love*. She takes us on a journey to find our true and authentic selves. A must-read for all who struggle to love self to the fullest."

-Mary Blythers Farmer
Founder, Sister Circle Book Club,
Fayetteville, North Carolina

"*Extracting the Good: The Importance of Self-Love* is a must-read, especially for young women. It teaches us to embrace the goodness we bring to the world. This book gives a fresh take on concepts such as prosperity. Bravo, Alberta Lampkins!"

-Camille Williams, Buffalo, New York

ACKNOWLEDGMENTS

With a grateful heart, I am thankful for the many blessings bestowed upon me from an incomparably great Creator whose bounties I cannot deny.

I sincerely thank my family for encouraging me to follow my heart. To my husband, Al, I can't thank you enough for always "covering" us and being the man God created you to be; for me, I love you with all my heart. To my daughter, Alexis, you are a wonderful blessing, and as I wrote this book, I thought of you in each chapter; your strength is my motivation; keep being exactly who the Creator made you to be, and keep shining.

To my son, Ahmad, words cannot express how encouraged I am by your genius and the mastery of your mind expressed through your music; stay true to yourself and keep those verses flowing – you inspire me, and I can't wait to see your family and your career grow. To my grandson, Elijah, what a beautiful gift the Creator has given us; you are an awesome young man, and I pray that you will pick this book up, read it, and keep moving toward your greatest potential; you are on the rise.

To my sisters, Marjorie and Benita, and my brother Sam – thank you for ensuring we continue to honor our parents by sticking together; I love each of you. To my mother and father-in-love, Trudy and Clarence, thank you for listening when I needed to get my thoughts and ideas out; you are the perfect encouragers. To my brother-in-love, Robert, thanks for being a great hype man, seeing the vision of my many projects, and always being an encouragement.

To my sister-in-love, Camille, thank you for standing ready to be the friend and sister I need. And, to all my many beloved uncles, aunts, nieces, nephews, cousins, and more, know that I love you all!

Special appreciation to my beloved *Sister Circle Book Club* members, especially Mary Blythers Farmer, Pam Farmer, Jo Dessaw, and friend and author Suzetta Perkins – I truly appreciate your love and support!

And thank you to my many amazing friends for sharing my journey. Lakesha Parker, Zena Orr, Tina Thomas, Valencia Warren-Gibbs, and Currentra Kinsey, you each know how much I love and appreciate you; we are sisters and friends for life!

Dedication

In memory of my mother and father, Sam and Macieon Hairston; not a day goes by that I don't think of you and thank the Creator for blessing me with two parents who loved me unconditionally. I would not be who I am today without the love you poured into me – may you rest in peace. Your memory lives forever in me.

I also dedicate this book to the memory of my sister, Agnes – I was always trying to wear your shoes and match your style; thank you for showing me that it is okay to be myself. You were one of a kind!

May we each find the divine beneficence within us and embrace our uniqueness.

He created man. He taught him expression. Which then of the bounties of the Creator will you deny?

-Surah 55

Table of Contents

Introduction 1

Chapter 1
    Pearls (Your Uniqueness) 3

Chapter 2
    Rewards of Goodness 26

Chapter 3
    Prosperity 36

Chapter 4
    Courage 48

Chapter 5
    Love 66

Chapter 6
    Divine Creativity 82

Chapter 7
    Bringing Balance 92

Chapter 8
    Strengthening Relationships 112

Chapter 9
    Wisdom through Experiences 126

Chapter 10
    Do for self (Self-love) 138

Conclusion 155

The more you praise and Celebrate your life, the more there is in life to celebrate.

-Oprah Winfrey

INTRODUCTION

There is always something to be thankful for every day of your life. Regardless of your condition, as dim as it can appear on occasion, there is continuously something that would merit appreciation. Frequently, the best times to be thankful are during the most troublesome times.

Gratitude is a strong emotion. At the point when you are genuinely appreciative, it's difficult to feel fear, stress, uneasiness, or any of those pessimistic feelings that stop you from fulfilling your true destiny. It would be best if you allowed gratitude to dominate. Go on a walk, run, or sit outside (preferably in nature), bring your journal if you have it, and begin to flood your mind with the astounding things in your life. You can ask yourself: 'What have I done for myself and others? What extraordinary impact am I placing on the planet? What am I thankful for?' The less complex things you can find appreciation in, the more frequently you'll wind up immersed in them.

Go out and connect with individuals who add value to life. Begin with the least difficult way of showing gratitude: Invest your energy with your loved ones and those who love you. Be there with them and be present. There is no sign of affection, appreciation, and thoughtfulness more authentic than being there. It is as basic as that.

When did you last feel thankful for something? What was it? For what reason did you feel grateful? How could you offer your thanks? All the more critically, how did your gratitude influence different aspects of your life? Did you feel some additional pep in your step? Could it be said that you were more joyful? Did you have a more hopeful outlook toward the future?

We will discuss these and others in this book to help you reflect on the acts of appreciation, kindness, and self-love.

CHAPTER 1

PEARLS (YOUR UNIQUENESS)

'Such as I am, I am a Precious Gift.' -
Zora Neale Hurston

Everybody is unique in their own specific manner. Most individuals try to mix with the crowd but often feel lost because they hide their true selves. Some others take their uniqueness, stand apart as different, and utilize their exceptional persona to make and experience the necessary existence. On the off chance that you are prepared to stand apart from the group, you first need to embrace what makes you one of a kind. You want to acknowledge your identity without expecting to squeeze into a mark of whom you ought to be. Realize that you will stand apart once you embrace all that makes you unique and will likewise be in complete control of your life and happiness.

Every person is a fascinating individual composed of a mosaic of character traits, educational encounters, information, and feelings. Each individual possesses a unique perspective and worldview, generally filled by how they've encountered and explored the world. Regardless of your life's path, the journey transforms and shapes how you collaborate with your present reality. But you must understand that you are not sentenced to a specific result.

The characteristics that contribute to your uniqueness and intriguing personality can be sharpened, refined, and developed as you advance in your life's journey. So, what truly makes you remarkable? While only one of the accompanying things can make a person exceptional, if you join them together, you can see precisely how novel we all are.

Encounters

Your past and future encounters undeniably have the greatest influence on shaping your identity as a unique individual. Each experience helps determine how you will ultimately interact with the world and the people within it. For instance, an individual with pessimistic encounters might feel restless and protective when confronted with circumstances like those in which they got injured or while attempting to avoid future hurt.

What's more? We often actively seek out specific encounters to help us understand the world, our interactions with the people around us, and how best to live a blissful and content life. However, that doesn't imply that our experiences confine or restrict us because even some negative encounters have slivers of insight we can use to find a better path, settle on better choices, and seek a surer future.

A unique set of experiences marks each person's life. Everyone encounters a variety of situations in their day-to-day activities, even when they share the same workplace or spend time together. For example, I spent a week with my closest friends, whom I fondly refer to as my "Sister Circle," at the exquisite Moon Palace resort in Ocho Rios, Jamaica. Although we spent about seven days together and generally did the same things, we encountered the time there somewhat differently and had two one-of-a-kind encounters that impacted us in various ways. These diverse experiences, spanning our entire and even daily lives, contribute to making us the unique individuals we all are today.

Perception

Is there anyone on Earth who sees the world the exact way you do? Most unlikely!

No other person has experienced the same 24 hours a day, seven days a week, and 365 days a year as you. No one has faced life the same way you have. You are the only person with the same assortment of experiences you have. Therefore, your perception of things and life, in general, is mainly your own.

That is why it is crucial to maintain an openness to the thoughts and perspectives of others. Instead of hastily categorizing them as right or wrong, engage in dialogues that help fill the gaps and further develop your unique understanding of the world. A trade of thoughts with a mindful individual with a different worldview can broaden your horizons and expand your knowledge and wisdom. Therefore, paying attention to others and actively sharing your viewpoints and emotions is essential.

Your perspective on life may not necessarily align with that of anyone else. While there may be occasions where you and a friend see things from a similar perspective, in general, your opinion will often diverge from those of others. Perception plays a significant role in how we experience and interpret things, shaping what makes each of us unique.

For example, I recently had a conversation with a friend via text. I shared a story that didn't sit well with her. I thought it was harmless and didn't attach much importance to it. Despite knowing my friend and having an understanding of what I could or couldn't share with her, she insisted that what I said upset her. We had different interpretations of something seemingly straightforward, influenced by our daily experiences, which impacted our outlook on the conversation. I picked up the phone and called her. Once I listened to her explanation of why it upset her, I could see things differently and gained greater respect.

Convictions

Your conviction encompasses your life experiences and perceptions. You hold what you consider to be true based on what you have encountered in life. Your convictions about yourself, others, the world, what's good and bad, and all other things are never, in a million years, going to perfectly align with another person's convictions.

Moreover, beliefs are not static and can change over the

long haul. This means that even if you currently share a conviction or belief with someone, you may diverge in your beliefs from here on out.

Imagination

Creativity is a fascinating aspect of human expression, encompassing numerous forms and manifestations. It entails various artistic endeavors that engage the creative side of your brain, from painting and attracting to dancing and singing. However, creativity also extends to other spheres, such as crafting a beautiful piece of art, building a bookshelf with your hands, or preparing a satisfying meal.

Every person possesses unique and innovative gifts that are influenced by their vision of excellence. However, beauty is not always complex or intricate; sometimes, it can be found in the simplest things.

Creative talents come in diverse forms; everyone has one creative gift, talent, or another. Some of us excel as motivational speakers, others as designers, some are skilled at pottery, and some possess a remarkable ability to imagine and envision things.

According to Lynne Levesque, Ed. D., there are eight distinct creative gifts that individuals can draw from. These gifts include the swashbuckler, the guide, the pilot, the designer, the wayfarer, the negotiator, the writer, and the visionary. Each of these categories represents a unique set of skills and attributes that contribute to individual creativity. Within these groups, we each branch out in unique ways, adding our personal touch, perspective, and beliefs. It is this uniqueness that sets us apart from each other, even within the same creative gift category.

Genetics

Indeed, our genetic makeup also contributes to significant differences among us. Research has shown that we are approximately 90 to nearly 100% genetically diverse, owing to the variations in our genes and the number of duplications of those genes. Even very little alterations in our genetic code can profoundly affect how our genes are utilized or expressed. While delving into the details of genetics may become complex, it is clear that no two individuals are genetically identical.

Body

Each person's body is unique and carries its distinct characteristics. It's a remarkable fact that everyone carries their weight differently and comes in various shapes and sizes. It is evident when we look around and observe the diverse range of body types. However, there is a societal expectation that we should all look a particular way, which is unrealistic.

Those who embrace and celebrate their unique bodies always stand out from the crowd. Whether you are slender, pleasantly plump, short, tall, or fall somewhere in between, these differences remind you of the incredible diversity among individuals.

Connections

The connections we form have a profound influence on our lives. They shape our self-perception and impact how we engage with the world around us. No individual can claim to have the same connections as another person. Even if two individuals are friends who associate with the same group of people, their relationships within that group will still differ in some way or another.

Some individuals naturally connect with others more easily than others. Some people share specific beliefs that bind them together in a unique way. Meanwhile, conflicts and disagreements over small matters can affect the dynamics of some other relationships. Collectively, the variety of relationships we have in our lives contributes significantly to what makes each person unique.

What You Love To Do

How would you jump at an opportunity to have fun? It is a common icebreaker question that can provide valuable insights into your personality and interests and help others get to know you better. While hobbies alone do not define a person, they do offer a glimpse into the activities that bring you joy and fulfillment.

For example, whether you enjoy reading mystery novels, binge-watching shows on Netflix, engaging in sports, participating in humanitarian efforts, gardening, cooking, or teaching, these choices reflect something about your uniqueness, your values, and how you seek happiness and meaning in life. It also implies that trying and taking on new hobbies can help you explore other parts of what makes you exceptional and assist you in working on your development and self-improvement.

Knowledge

It is an obvious truth that we all possess a distinct knowledge base, influenced by our beliefs, social background, personal awareness, experiences, and mental capacity. No two individuals are riding on the same level of insight; this emphasizes the importance of collaboration in problem-solving. What you understand or discover can contribute to expanding the awareness of others while enhancing yours also.

Experiencing The World

We all possess five prevailing faculties that greatly contribute to our uniqueness. Our perception of the world, our experiences, and what we hear can significantly impact how we perceive and utilize these senses.

For instance, during my trip with my friends to Jamaica, some of them were intrigued by the experience of horseback riding in the ocean. While they focused on the thrill of the activity, I, being not accustomed to riding a horse and hesitant to try it, was excited for them, but directed my attention toward appreciating the natural beauty of Jamaica. At the same time, some others were more focused on the happenings in and around the resort. As a result, our sensory experiences varied. We heard different sounds, smelled different scents, saw different sights, and even tasted different flavors, all influenced by our perspectives and choices.

Another example can be seen in our preferences for different types of music. While some individuals love Rhythm and Blues (R&B), others derive joy from jazz or gospel music. Our musical preferences are often closely tied to our life experiences and personal beliefs. One person may have grown up listening to Hip Hop with their close friends, while another may have developed an interest in traditional or gospel music through their parents, aunts, or uncles.

Behavior

An individual's behavior significantly shapes their perception of life and how they interact with others. Whether you have a positive or negative attitude, it can have a powerful impact on the people around you, influencing the overall direction of their experiences and interactions with you. This forms the foundation of personal development and motivational resources that emphasize how your attitude can greatly influence your achievements in life.

Since individuals with an inspirational perspective often avoid those with impartial or negative mentalities, your demeanor is framed by your close-to-home scene, except if you settle on an effective decision to transform it into something beneficial and conducive to a happier present and future.

Your Propensities

We often engage in propensities with great regularity, which play a crucial role in helping us figure out and develop different aspects of ourselves. Engaging in a persistent habit of consuming unhealthy food and neglecting exercise can lead to a sedentary lifestyle and poor physical well-being. Conversely, a beneficial routine of brushing your teeth twice a day and flossing can maintain a healthy and pain-free mouth.

Forming propensities such as reading, meditating, exercising, or exploring new things can improve your psychological health and overall well-being. The words of Carl Jung, "You are what you do, not what you say you'll do," resonate deeply in addressing how our actions and habits determine the person we ultimately become.

Your Enthusiasm

Enthusiasm is a remarkable aspect of the human experience. It encompasses a wide range of things that ignite our excitement and fervor, such as art, nature, and the well-being of humanity. Having passions in life can provide a sense of purpose and direction towards goals or experiences that have the potential to create a lasting impact and make history. It is often the things that stir the deepest emotions within us that call us to pursue a higher purpose beyond ourselves, even when we may find ourselves in seemingly unfavorable situations. Our passions and enthusiasm can serve as a source of inspiration and motivation, driving us to strive for meaningful contributions and positive change in the world.

Understanding your interests can lead you to find your purpose in life. Try not to allow your interests to chill off to nothing. Stir up those hobbies now and again so they proceed to consume you and enlighten your way. We are passionate and enthusiastic beings, and as a whole, we have something unique and significant to add to the world. It may only require an investment to extract it.

Taste

The way we 'taste' things is essential for detecting our general surroundings, and it's important to recognize that everyone's perception of taste is unique. Several factors influence how we taste things.

First, our early experiences, especially during childhood, shape our preferences for different foods. The flavors we become accustomed to during this developmental stage can influence our future food choices and preferences.

However, the way we 'taste' has a connection with the number of taste buds we have, the tangible limits those taste buds have, and the way our brain interprets the signals from these taste buds and sensory receptors.

Some individuals may have more taste buds and heightened sensory sensitivity, allowing them to enjoy and savor the flavors of any meal thoroughly. On the other hand, those with fewer taste buds may have a less intense experience of flavors when eating a meal.

What do you like? What do you dislike? We all have preferences that play a significant role in forming our character and influencing our choices. However, we can always settle on some shared interest with others on what comprises quality or excellence. Your preferences will impact many decisions throughout everyday life, from the food you eat to the kind of people you prefer to have relationships with.

Exploring the diverse range of preferences of the world is an enriching experience that allows us to extend our perspectives, learn new things, and continue to create and grow personally as well as professionally. Keeping an open mind and embracing the preferences of others can introduce us to a multitude of incredible things.

Character

Your character comprises a range of attributes, including your demeanor, mentality, contemplations, convictions, reactions, and conduct. It uniquely reflects who you are and strongly affects how people interact with you and what they think of you. When people associate with you, they form impressions based on your character, showing how exceptional it is.

For instance, through your interactions with someone, you may see them as vibrant, tranquil, insightful, friendly, annoying, or rude based on their reception towards you, their demeanor, and their actions. These aspects collectively contribute to one's character.

The events that shape your character begin at conception and continually evolve. It is influenced by a multitude of life events and experiences, both positive and negative. Each significant moment, whether it be a triumph or setback, a victory or a disappointment, a snapshot of solidarity or a shortcoming, contributes to forming your identity. All the information you have gathered over the years has become ingrained in your mind and influences your character and the decisions you make as you navigate life's journey.

Your character and identity are truly unique to you. The combination of information, experiences, and insights that shape your being is unparalleled. No one else will have encountered the same circumstances as you or have interpreted them with the same emotions and thoughts. No one will settle for the same decisions that you make. The makeup of your character is exclusively yours.

Corresponding Propensities

Each person has a unique style of how they communicate. The way we express ourselves mirrors our thoughts, considerations, convictions, and character.

Some individuals are open and vocal about whatever is at the forefront of their thoughts, while others are more reserved and like to keep their private matters to themselves. Some individuals are brilliant at interpreting nonverbal cues and effectively using body language to convey their messages, while others see nothing past the spoken words and may downplay the significance of non-verbal communication in a conversation.

Humor

Humor is subjective, and what one person finds "amusing," another person may not. For example, I don't find *The Simpsons* entertaining, yet many people connect with the show, which is what's genuinely going on with humor. What we find amusing often relates to what we have encountered or experienced and how we see life. And keeping in mind that humorists can address ordinary things that a large portion of us can connect with.

Objectives

As individuals, we all have various goals and longings from day to day. Even if we share a similar objective, for example, running a successful organization, the degree of our needs and our motivation towards that goal will differ greatly. You may prioritize financial success and aim to earn a specific amount of money or prioritize positively impacting others rather than just accumulating wealth.

Your goals in life affect how you spend your time and invest your energy. The activities and efforts we invest more of our time, energy, and exertion on often reflect our priorities and what we consider important and influence what we offer in return and take from the world.

Setting goals, whether they are short-term, medium-term, or long-term, provides us with direction and motivation when we feel lost or unsure of our path. You can get more out of your life, develop personally, and find a clearer view when you set goals for yourself. Journaling can be a valuable tool in this process, as it allows you to freely express your thoughts, map out your needs, and nurture your plan to achieve your goals.

Instinct

Some individuals possess heightened instincts that guide their daily decision-making process, while others rely more on reasoning and logical analysis before reaching a decision. However, various factors influence how intuitive a person is, and the brain is one of them.

Individuals with a more grounded right brain hemisphere often appear more intuitive because they can easily make connections between things. The right brain hemisphere is associated with visual processing and creative thinking, while the left-brain hemisphere is known for analytical and logical thinking.

While the study of neuroscience doesn't fully support the

notion that we function solely from the left or right brain, there is no denying that our daily experiences and the approaches we have learned shape how much emphasis we place on one side over the other.

Ability To Always Be Yourself

Have you ever wondered what makes you remarkable? It is your willingness to accept your identity and stand out from the crowd. Being different is an astounding feat, as many people are scared to embrace their uniqueness and lean toward their feelings. Some are hesitant to flaunt their actual character and how they associate with the world.

I have often encountered situations where individuals agree with others to fit in. And it tends to manifest in the smallest of forms. For instance, someone might purchase a non-branded handbag even though they genuinely desire the latest *Michael Kors* designer handbag just so they can conform to some societal standards. The non-branded handbag may be just as nice, but one may feel inadequate because it is not a *Michael Kors* designer bag.

The most extraordinary individuals in the world are those who wholeheartedly embrace their authentic selves. When you encounter such individuals, acknowledge and celebrate them, for they exemplify what it means to live an enthusiastic and unrestrained life. They are destined to fulfill their unique purpose in life.

In all your uniqueness, you might share certain components with others, like similar cooking styles and leisure activities, or hold comparable convictions or assessments to others. What makes an individual different from all others is a blend of all these things that allow you to be your genuine self.

In your individuality, you may share certain elements with others, such as similar styles, hobbies, or shared beliefs and opinions. However, what truly sets you apart from everyone else is not these individual components only but the unique blend of these elements you possess.

I want you to know you are one of a kind, and there's not even a shadow of a doubt.

you are enough

EXTRACTING THE GOOD: THE IMPORTANCE OF SELF-LOVE

NOTES TO SELF

_____

_____

_____

_____

_____

_____

_____

_____

_____

CHAPTER 2

REWARDS OF GOODNESS

"Does goodness only yield goodness as its reward?"

"Should I strive to live ethically?"

"Why should I consider being moral?"

EXTRACTING THE GOOD: THE IMPORTANCE OF SELF-LOVE

"Is it wise for me to prioritize moral behavior for my well-being and future, or would I be better off being corrupt as long as I can pull it off and not get caught?

Combining personal satisfaction with a heightened sense of self-confidence, it becomes evident that being a morally deficient person is horrible. Let's explore some compelling reasons for this perspective. Here are the benefits of being decent.

1. *Being unpleasant is just awful both for you and others.*

    Some people have propagated a misguided notion that being unpleasant or shameless can be good for anyone, particularly if you can "gain from it."

    However, there are a few valid justifications to refute this notion. The foremost reason is that being unpleasant or corrupt is inherently self-slighting and makes it difficult to envision contentment with a sense of pride. Here's a key argument:

    Being morally upright (or distinguished) is essential for cultivating self-confidence, and self-confidence is crucial for experiencing genuine happiness.

2. *Being morally upright is important for your*

happiness.

Certainly, a comprehensive defense of this viewpoint requires more than can be provided in a brief paragraph. However, it is relatively easy to recognize how acts such as lying, cheating, stealing, or generally engaging in unethical behavior are incompatible with cultivating unwavering self-confidence.

Being moral is the optimal path to developing self-confidence. You can only have confidence in yourself when you honestly perceive who you truly are. This means that self-confidence requires self-

awareness. Furthermore, morally upright individuals can make unbiased and fair self-evaluations.

3. *Being a decent human allows you to recognize and appreciate all the valuable things that hold worth in the world.*

Part of what distinguishes greatness is the ability to discern what is excellent and valuable from what is not. Great qualities require appreciating and cherishing what deserves our love and attention rather than focusing on things that hold no merit or value in our lives.

4. *Being moral entails taking great consideration for yourself.*

   No, it doesn't mean being selfish or improper. It also doesn't mean you should act like you're the only significant being on earth, as this line of thought always leads to a loss of purpose and direction in life. It means allowing yourself to BE BETTER to and for yourself.

5. *Being decent allows you to be energetic and be the best version of yourself.*

   You can only be the best version of yourself, so showcase who you are and don't try to embody someone else. Don't permit worthless negativities, like regular interruptions of feelings, wants, and needs to disrupt you from being your best self.

6. *Being decent to yourself and others requires courage at all times, notwithstanding risk, distress, dismissal, and depression.*

   You have the power to bring the reality you want for your life into existence. And boldness plays a crucial role in this process by helping you break down barriers, navigate through distractions, and seize opportunities that usher you into being the best you can be.

7. *Being decent gives you space to gain insight and experience for your future.*
Profound insight is a quality that may only be available to some who have keen wisdom. However, we all can be in every way discerning and gain insight into the "main issue," if we begin to pay attention to the things that hold value. So, being decent and morally upright helps us spread the right qualities by cherishing the right things.

8. *Being decent implies being an admirer of everything great.*

If you are an admirer of great things, automatically, you'd cherish excellence. If you appreciate greatness, you can be cherished by great people too. What more could anyone possibly desire over being cherished by a great individual you admire?

9. *Most importantly, simply being a great person can lead you to a genuinely cheerful life.*

Can you remember the last time you did something thoughtful for someone? If you can, congratulations.

You're fantastic, and the world is fortunate to have you. However, if you're still trying to remember, you can relax. You're in good company.

We experience so much in a day, and we shuffle countless things consistently that sometimes, we find it hard to take care of our needs, let alone the needs of others. We experience a daily reality such that desire, assurance, and a ferocious demeanor are valued over being thoughtful, tranquil, and noble.

From an early age, we are told to approach life with self-resilience. However, this emphasis on self-reliance often makes us overlook the importance of thoughtfulness in adulthood. That's why we need to explore its meaning, understand its significance, and why we need to incorporate it into our daily lives. When we practice it sincerely, it has the power to change our lives for the better.

WHAT IS GENEROSITY?

Generosity is the act of selflessly doing something for someone without expecting anything in return. It comes from a compassionate mindset and is, in most cases, driven by care. For instance, an illustration of generosity is going out of your way to help an elderly neighbor by picking up a few items from the grocery store, knowing she can't drive to the shop to get them herself.

The Advantages of Being Generous

Incorporating goodness, consideration, and generosity into your daily routine is important for several reasons. Here are some of these advantages:

1. Being kind decidedly affects your general prosperity.
2. It eases anxiety.
3. It helps you get rid of feelings of hopelessness, exclusion, and aggression.
4. Being caring gives your unconquerable framework an enormous lift.
5. It can decrease the impact of any medical problems you have.
6. It advances quiet, loosening up contemplations.
7. It encourages a positive and hopeful world viewpoint.
8. It helps you build a healthy identity, self-worth, and self-assurance.
9. Kind individuals often carry on with longer and more joyful lives than narrow-minded individuals.

So, as well as helping others, effectively rehearsing the craft of benevolence can work on your own physical and profound well-being. Essentially, it's a mutually beneficial arrangement. Try this. Make a special effort to be caring to others for seven days. If you don't begin resting easier thinking about yourself in three days, you may want to try it for another seven days (smile).

Practicing the Art of Thoughtfulness

How can you become a beacon of sheer thoughtfulness? It's quite simple and requires a touch of thought and action.

Start by identifying the people who are close or dear to you, such as your family members, friends, colleagues, or neighbors. Reflect on their preferences, interests, and needs and consider the simple yet meaningful gestures that would bring them joy and light up their day.

Everything necessary is one little sacrificial activity. It could be buying flowers for your mom or daughter, getting your colleagues their favorite expresso, assisting a friend with a home improvement project, or offering to help a family member with lawn mowing.

The potential outcomes are unfathomable, so don't hesitate for even a moment to think about how you can communicate your kind and little thoughtful gestures.

Why not stretch your thoughtfulness to outsiders to kick things up a notch? For example, offer to pay for a meal for a stranger in a restaurant, brighten the day of the people you meet with a pleasant smile, or surprise your co-workers with a treat to some coffee or donuts. Let your imagination run wild and discover new ways to spread kindness and generosity in the world around you.

Remember, giving is receiving. So, get your benevolence on and watch your life-altering for the better in a few days. You will love it, I guarantee!

Overall, you benefit significantly more by being a decent human since you will do yourself and the world an extraordinary deed daily. It doesn't cost anything to hold entryways and greet someone pleasantly. The benefits are a great deal more due to the joy you'd be giving others, particularly yourself.

EXTRACTING THE GOOD: THE IMPORTANCE OF SELF-LOVE

NOTES TO SELF

CHAPTER 3

PROSPERITY

'I'm fulfilled in what I do. I never thought that a lot of money or fine clothes — the finer things in life would make you happy. My concept of happiness is to be filled in a spiritual sense.'
-Coretta Scott King

EXTRACTING THE GOOD: THE IMPORTANCE OF SELF-LOVE

Is accomplishing success only about money and satisfaction?

Undoubtedly, money and happiness are important aspects of life. However, exploring what else contributes to a truly prosperous and fulfilling life is equally important. Much of what we have been led to believe about prosperity and how to attain it is off track.

Only some are adequately misconceived to accept that doing well implies that we have an overabundance of money. Instead, success's fundamental parts - money, joy, and maintainability - should be aligned to continue a prosperous life.

It is a misconception to think that the overabundance of money alone equates to success. Instead, true success encompasses the fundamental components of money, joy, and maintainability.

How would we characterize Prosperity?

    1. MONEY.

In this conversation, we acknowledge that money is important for supporting our goals. Acquiring "enough" money is significant to achieve success. But how much money is "enough"?

The concept of "enough" differs exclusively for everyone as it aligns with our financial aspirations while upholding our values and standards. This limit will keep us from intruding into a mentality where money overshadows and compromises our core values and standards.

While our boundaries may evolve with time, it is important to remember that money alone does not guarantee true success. If we compromise our integrity in pursuit of financial gain, we must ask ourselves if the monetary benefit is worth sacrificing our self-respect.

2. JOY.

After the question, "How much money is enough?" comes "Am I adequately joyful?"

Think about these accompanying parts of joy.

- Perspective – having good sentiments about yourself and the world.
- Legitimacy – carrying on with life with our most profound convictions, values, and standards, keeping in mind that our profits align with our interests and

reason.
- Responsibility – sticking to what matters the most, like family and connections.
- Well-being – chasing after an overflow of well-being as a primary concern, soul and body.

3. MAINTAINABILITY

This is the most neglected part of success. The accompanying four inquiries call for reflection on how realistic we genuinely trust our current or future success to be. To ensure maintainability, the first question on your mind should be, "Do I feel good about what I do?"

Some people become scared when they make money from doing something beyond their usual range of skills. It takes courage to align your sources of income with what genuinely inspires you and gives meaning to your life. This might require a significant change for some, involving an investment. However, when you love your work because you are passionate about it, you become more mindful of nuances, more committed to growth, and more valuable. Most importantly, working from your core protects you from being crushed by occasional setbacks or disappointments.

Another crucial question to consider is, can I sustain the required effort over the long term? Do you have the enthusiasm and interest to keep at it for a long time? Wearing out or compromising your well-being by engaging in something that drains you is not a wise decision, as any success you achieve through such means will eventually fade. If you wake up each day feeling anxious about your work, it becomes impossible to derive joy from it, let alone achieve success. Someone passionate about the same work will outshine you.

Furthermore, assessing if your achievements are morally sound, valuable to others, and aligned with natural principles is important. You must not base your success on monetary benefits alone. Is your moral compass genuinely pointing north? Are your intentions ethically sound? Are you benefiting at the detriment of others?

Does it offer lasting value? There is no room for get-rich-quick schemes or easy money scams in genuine prosperity. Reasonable and sustainable prosperity is built on the law of the harvest, which says, "You reap what you sow." So, what seeds are you planting? Will you be happy with what you reap? Will your harvest contribute positively to the environment in which you work and live?

EXTRACTING THE GOOD: THE IMPORTANCE OF SELF-LOVE

The journey to success and prosperity begins with questions and insightful planning. One of the first things you must do is assess your ongoing convictions and activities fairly. Give thoughts to the following:

- *What is my lifestyle like?*
- *How much money do I need to keep up with my ideal lifestyle?*
- *How can I nurture and maintain the primary relationships in my daily life?*
- *How significant is the feeling of true prosperity?*
- *How much activity do I aim for each week?*
- *How do I work on my reputation, self-confidence, and courage?*
- *What brings me the most joy, and why?*
- *What level of natural, economic living do I plan to achieve?*
- *Does money make me happier?*

Spread Love

The more love you express to others, the more love you will experience. As human beings, we have an innate desire to form bonds with others. Show that you appreciate your bonds and connections with others through small acts of kindness and thoughtful gestures.

Experience from Life

Sometimes, negative encounters can foster self-improvement and a positive turn of events. So, try not to allow one awful experience to diminish your confidence. Be noble and acknowledge the messes you have made. We can all always learn from past experiences and use the lessons as stepping stones for personal growth.

Show Regard

If you regard others, they are likely to reciprocate. In general, treating others the same way you want to be treated is important. While this saying may be old, the principle is rarely obsolete.

Be Mindful

Assume total control over your activities. Act with sound judgment and always show love and regard to everyone. Remember, you achieve more when you give more.

Be Good

Carry on with an authentic and respectable life. Be the fair, genuine, and conscious individual you want others to be to you.

Accept Your Errors

Accepting your mistakes is a sign of maturity and courage. As humans, none of us are perfect (except, of course, the Creator). Many people will respect you for acknowledging your wrongs or mistakes, making them keen to learn from you.

Pardon

Do not allow seemingly insignificant issues to disrupt your life and tamper with great relationships. Relationships hold immense value in personal and professional spheres, so it is important not to take them for granted. Therefore, when small conflicts arise, do not let them destroy your relationship. Instead, forgive and move on.

Change

Be open to change! Embracing change can be challenging,

especially when we are unsure about how to adapt to new circumstances. However, change has the potential to bring growth and development into our lives, pushing us to explore things that we ordinarily feel uncomfortable with.

Figure out how to Tune in

The art of listening can pique the interest of some people. Sometimes, we feel we are "tuned in," but our focus is primarily on the thoughts swirling in our minds. Take a stab at listening carefully and be fully present in the moment. By tuning in to others, we have the opportunity to learn from their perspectives and gain a deeper understanding of their thoughts and emotions. By practicing tuning in, you can enhance your communication skills, comprehend others more effectively and maintain meaningful connections with others.

Make Room for Overflow

Create a safe space at home where adoration and harmony prevail. By fostering an environment of love, we provide opportunities for joy, overflow, and growth to flourish.

Remember, when you show love and kindness to others, you also receive noteworthy satisfaction and rewards in return.

Practice Quiet Reflection

Invest energy in reflecting at least once a day. This allows you to ponder your day and connect it with the broader context of your life. This serves as a foundation for your personal growth, abundance, and flourishing.

Give Yourself to Individuals

In every relationship, the love and care you show hold more significance than what you expect to gain. By giving yourself to others without anticipating anything in particular, you ultimately experience the greatest fulfillment and rewards.

"Try to be a rainbow in someone's cloud." Maya Angelou

The most well-known conviction, whether we believe it or not, is that a high income is directly connected with happiness. We generally believe that the more money we have, the more joyful and fulfilled we will be. It does minimal good to challenge this conviction, even though, through experience, we see that this isn't often the case.

What we can say regarding the connection between money and satisfaction is that money indeed does, without a doubt, makes us happier, yet just to the degree that it liberates us from stress and anxiety associated with meeting basic needs like food and shelter. When happiness is related to these basic needs, money is great.

More than money

Success is associated with the drive to improve one's circumstances. Often, this improvement is connected to money; fortunately, assurance and money can work together. The quest for money is praiseworthy and decent when driven by value-aligned intentions rather than mere love for money.

Finally, figure out what prosperity means to you. The more discerning you are about your conditions, wants, and objectives, the more accurate your understanding and definition of success will be.

NOTES TO SELF

_____

_____

_____

_____

_____

_____

_____

_____

_____

_____

CHAPTER 4

COURAGE

If you fall behind, run faster. Never give up, never surrender, and rise against the odds.
-Jesse Jackson

If you're like most people, you may likely compare mental fortitude with bravery, but that is a flawed understanding. Mental fortitude goes beyond mere bravery. It is making a move despite the trepidation you may feel. Fortitude is the willingness to respond with bravery even in the face of discomfort and anxiety that may try to hold you back.

One of the most powerful ways to be bold is to understand what you're afraid of and then refuse to let that fear incapacitate you. Allowing fear to dictate your actions can hinder your progress, prevent you from taking risks, and hold you back from seizing opportunities. However, being bold means facing your fears head-on, following your dreams, and not allowing them to limit your potential.

To be more courageous, there are several approaches you can take to strengthen your fortitude and make the most of every circumstance. Here is an overview of what you need to know about bravery and some practical tips to help you carry on with life infused with bravery.

Advantages of Fortitude

Being more courageous helps you to respond appropriately to challenges and take action. Overcoming fears and anxieties requires effort and dedication. Nonetheless, boldness helps you thoroughly consider things, analyze the dangers and rewards, and take action despite the inevitable apprehension.

Also, courage enables you to pursue things that are important to you. It strengthens your confidence and allows you to trust in your abilities. However, it is necessary to understand that mental fortitude is not the absence of fear.

Sometimes, feeling a little bit of fear can be beneficial because it prompts you to pause and evaluate risks appropriately. Do not beat yourself up or assume you are not brave when you feel bouts of fear. Courage is not the absence of fear; it is your innate ability to face your fears and take action appropriately.

Moreover, as you continually confront your fears, you gradually replace your fear-driven reactions with gutsy ones. Here are a few advantages of fortitude:

→ Being bold in the face of fear builds self-assurance.

→ Embracing courage allows for a broader perspective on the world.

→ Incorporating courage into your life inspires others to do the same.

→ Choosing to step out of your comfort zone and be more fearless brings balance and enriches your experiences.

→ Courage increases your effectiveness, and you are more likely to pursue your dreams and seize opportunities as they arise.

→ Embracing and integrating fortitude into your life enhances your satisfaction.

Suggestions on how to Feel More Fearless

Hopelessness is a potent force that encourages stagnation. Failure to see fear as what it is can hinder you from accomplishing your goals and seeking open doors. Many individuals have allowed fear to confine them within their familiar boundaries of mediocrity instead of exercising the courage to venture into new territories, regardless of the potential risks.

If you find that this situation resonates with your life, you might need to dig deeper to identify the areas in your daily life where you could be more courageous. For instance, do you need to actively pursue that promotion at work instead of solely relying on your efforts to be noticed? Or do you feel the need to speak up when a colleague is being belittled? There are likely numerous areas in your life. where you can exercise more courage. Here are a few suggestions to help you embrace courage and apply it to your life.

1. Keep a Sound Viewpoint

Too often, people believe that courage is an innate trait you either have or don't have. While it is true that some individuals may be more inclined to boldness, it does not mean that all hope is lost for you. Seeing courage as a muscle is a helpful perspective. Just as some individuals may be born with more well-defined muscles than others, everyone can improve their courage muscles through proper training and practice.

In like manner, it's vital to note that fear is not inherently bad. There are times when it is perfectly normal to feel afraid. For example, fear triggers your sensory system and survival instincts designed to protect you. Therefore, feeling a little scared when jostled by a stranger on a crowded train or during a thunderstorm is natural.

Instead of perceiving discomfort as something negative, consider it as a valuable opportunity to delve deeper into your identity and understand why you may feel fearful or reluctant to step out of your comfort zone. Acknowledging your fear and understanding its reason can provide insights into overcoming it or showing courage despite its presence.

Research shows that expressing your sentiments helps control your adverse reactions to fear. Also, it is essential to understand that voicing out your anxiety and fear doesn't make you vulnerable; rather, it makes you bold. Acknowledging your vulnerabilities and fears is not easy, but you are one bit nearer to being bold by doing so.

Therefore, acknowledge what is holding you back instead

of suppressing or denying your fear. By recognizing your fears—either through writing them down or opening up to a stronger individual—you are empowering yourself to be bold in the face of fear.

2. Recognize Your Strength

About living a life filled with courage, it is beneficial to start by identifying your strengths and areas where you have experienced success. Research shows that individuals who recognize and cultivate their strengths tend to be more resilient, feel less discouraged, and experience greater happiness.

Also, a clear understanding of your strengths helps to boost your confidence, increasing your ability to overcome challenges and embrace courage. When you are positive about your abilities, you are more inclined to seize opportunities that come your way.

Furthermore, when dealing with fear and the need to cultivate more courage, it is normal to zero in on your shortcomings and weaknesses. However, doing so can undermine your ability to be bold. Therefore, reflecting on your strengths and accomplishments is crucial to build your confidence and fortitude.

3. Analyze Various Situations

When it comes to being courageous, it is helpful not to imagine only the worst-case scenario that could happen if you take a risk; also, think about what might happen if you didn't take any action at all. Often, comparing these two extremes is all you need to get past your feelings of fear because, in most cases, the potential benefits of taking action far outweigh the potential negative outcomes. If you consistently use correlations like these, you will develop resilience that prevents your fears from controlling you in the long run.

Additionally, you can engage in visualization exercises where you imagine yourself successfully handling something that you're afraid of. Visualize how you would navigate through different scenarios, including your responses or actions. These mental rehearsals allow you to practice being courageous without actually putting yourself in the situation until you feel prepared and confident.

4. Work on Leaving Your Usual range of familiarity

When you allow your fears to hinder you from experiencing something fun, pursuing your desires, or expressing your true self, you create a life that lacks true fulfillment. To change this, you must be intentional about making the necessary alterations for the better.

Building fortitude requires you to drive yourself beyond your comfort zone. Start by picking out a few situations that make you self-conscious but where the stakes are relatively low. For instance, you could strike up conversations with new people, dine alone at a restaurant, or volunteer for a small responsibility.

By gradually exposing yourself to these small challenges, you can become accustomed to being bold without taking on significant risks at the get-go. As you gain confidence and experience success in these smaller endeavors, you can gradually tackle more daunting challenges, like taking the lead on a project or spearheading a community initiative.

5. Diminish Your Pressure

Sometimes people experience fear or a lack of courage because they feel depleted and overwhelmed by the thought of taking on so much. If you feel overpowered, fatigued, or impeded, find a way to ease the pressure. That could mean taking a short vacation or some time off work in specific situations. Everybody needs a break once in a while. This way, if you feel weighed down by your attempts at boldness, it may lessen the pressure you feel.

It's almost impossible to be bold when you are overcome by worry and pressure.

6. Observe Brave Activities

Every act of courage deserves to be celebrated, especially if it is new for you. So, don't neglect to acknowledge and congratulate yourself when you act with courage despite feeling afraid. Experts agree that people who celebrate small victories are more likely to achieve long-term success.

You don't need to yell it from the rooftop or share it on social media, but take time to carefully reflect on your achievements and give yourself a pat on the back. You can consider keeping a journal of these little affirmations that you can revisit when you feel discouraged or afraid. Doing so will keep you from engaging in negative thoughts that suggest you will never be bold. It serves as a reminder of your past achievements and reinforces your belief in your ability to be courageous.

7. Welcome Disappointment

Most people fear disappointment because they associate it with negative emotions and potential setbacks. This fear leaves them stagnant, preventing them from taking necessary risks and pursuing their goals wholeheartedly. The fear of disappointment can make you confine yourself within a set of rigid rules and become a perfectionist while trying to avoid potential embarrassment or the shame that comes with failure.

Yet, it is crucial to maintain an open mindset toward disappointments. Daily, tell yourself that disappointment is okay and is allowed, especially if facing challenges beyond your normal range of action.

Furthermore, whenever seen as a welcome encounter rather than the worst situation imaginable, you can attempt new things despite the dangers implied. Disappointment provides an opportunity for personal development. It allows you to gain valuable insights, pivot your path, and test your resilience. By embracing disappointment as a welcome experience rather than the worst-case scenario, you can take up new challenges despite the potential risks.

It is never too late to take in courage. Fortitude is more

bravery you can cultivate through deliberate effort and practice. All it takes is the willingness to acknowledge your fears and the determination to choose action despite them.

Lastly, when you acknowledge your fears and take a proactive approach to address them and pursue your goals, you won't only cultivate courage; but increase your chances of overall success. View your fears as valuable opportunities to strengthen your courage muscles. With time, you will find yourself more willing to push through your discomfort and live the life you have longed for.

Advantages of Mental Fortitude

Being courageous accompanies a ton of advantages. The following are seven advantages that courageous individuals experience:

You have the power to live your dreams, explore uncharted territories, and take risks that others wouldn't dare if only you embraced courage. There may indeed be moments of frustration if you stumble along the way, but what if you succeed? Gracious, the rewards!

Embracing courage accompanies a ton of benefits. Here are seven advantages of being courageous:

EXTRACTING THE GOOD: THE IMPORTANCE OF SELF-LOVE

➤ *You can recognize your fears for what it is.*

The majority of people tend to deal with their fear in one of two ways. Some acknowledge it but mask it with other emotions and actions. Others hold onto their fear and magnify it.

When you embody courage, you can acknowledge your fear for what it is: your body's natural response to protect you. You'll consider that fear, adjust your actions accordingly, and move forward.

While you may not proceed if your safety is truly at risk and you have no defenses, in situations where it's a matter of fight or flight, you'll push through the difficult part in the pursuit of the rewards and fulfillment that lie on the other side.

➤ *You will experience continuous growth.*

Personal growth and development occur when you break out of your comfort zone. This concept has been extensively explored and discussed by influential speakers and covered in-depth in pioneering articles.

Life is meant to be lived, not simply repeated in predetermined patterns, often called "grooves."

Courage helps you leap out of this realm of complacency into spic and span. By doing so, you can continually grow and learn, embracing opportunities for personal and professional development.

- *Rejection won't upset you.*

    Overcoming the fear of rejection can significantly simplify your journey in life. The phrase "What will people think?" can cripple your dreams and ambitions. However, if you can detach yourself from the thoughts and opinions of strangers, you can wholeheartedly pursue your dreams and goals.

    Courage helps you understand that rejection is an inevitable part of achieving getting things done. Take J.K. Rowling, for example. Her Harry Potter book was rejected multiple times before it was finally published.

- *You will fully understand yourself.*

    Being "confident" doesn't mean that you are devoid of fear. Instead, it means that you possess the skills and abilities to confront and tackle any challenge that comes your way.

    When you dig deeper and identify your fears, you can

conquer any psychological deterrent you experience.

By taking the time to reflect on your fears, you begin to understand yourself better. Why do you experience this fear? Is it due to past experiences or anticipated outcomes? Have you observed it as a natural response ingrained in you?

➤ *You won't find it difficult to ask for help.*

Many individuals find it hard to ask for help from others because they fear dismissal or worry about irritating them. But, if you are bold, seeking help from others is easier. It comes as a natural inclination.

Courage may seem 'self-glorifying,' but it helps you understand that 'two heads are better than one.' As social beings, we might need help at one point or the other, and working together makes the job less complicated.

➤ *You won't lament your shortcomings.*

Lament is often a mix of complex emotions, particularly about missed opportunities. Nobody wants to look back on life and regret the decisions they never made.

You must have heard this thought-provoking question a few times, "When you're on your deathbed, will you be content with your decisions or regret what you didn't do?"

Taking risks might have consequences, but courage helps you to step out of your relaxed mode, reducing the chances of lingering on the thoughts of what could have been.

➤ *You'll have a lot to teach and tell others.*

Typically, courage shatters the boundaries that hold you back, allowing you to experience the world in its truest form. In the end, you'll have a lot of experiences and encounters that would have remained unexplored.

These experiences become the fabric of your life story, comprising your accomplishments no one thought was humanly possible, your failures, and the deadly risks you took.

Virtually every movie tells the story of a courageous person. Whether it's to wager with everything to get the young man or face the difficult situation to save the world, movies often highlight acts of courage because the movie is relatively boring and pointless without them.

Have a similar view as that courageous individual in the movie would. Take the first 15 seconds of trying anything new as the hardest. Once you review that short time frame, tell yourself you can make it to the end.

The confidence to confront significant challenges is a part of being courageous that others may admire. Many people long for the boldness to make choices that would bring them closer to their dreams, but they often get caught up in worrying about the details.

When you deliberately work on being bold, you can confront challenges head-on. You pursue your goals with determination and handle the outcomes, whether favorable or unfavorable.

However, being brave is not a walk in the park. It requires effort and resilience. It wouldn't be such an incredible quality to possess if it was easy.

let your Faith be bigger than your Fear ♥

NOTES TO SELF

_____

_____

_____

_____

_____

_____

_____

_____

_____

_____

CHAPTER 5

LOVE

You must've often heard, "Love yourself!" In the same way, it's safe to say you've come to learn that loving yourself is the best thing you can do for yourself. However, this chapter is for you if you have not come across the self-love ideologies and have no idea how to go about it.

What is confidence? What's its essence? And how can we be confident?

Confidence is about having a genuine and compassionate relationship with yourself. It involves treating yourself with empathy, generosity, perseverance, resilience, and curiosity. However, it doesn't mean that you're so self-indulgent that you deny the mistakes you've made. It's not about saying, "Oh, I love myself and believe I'm perfectly imperfect, so that could never be my fault!"

Confidence involves giving yourself room to make errors and forgiving yourself when you make those errors. It allows you to acknowledge your mistakes and take ownership of them. It doesn't mean being arrogant or, even worse, a narcissist who believes they are superior to everyone else and expects others to cater to their needs.

Confidence is about having faith in yourself, trusting your abilities, and believing in your worth.

Since the relationship you have with yourself is a lifelong, deep-rooted relationship, nurturing your self-worth should be your primary focus, besides nurturing your love for the Creator of your life.

What is the essence of Confidence?

You can only freely express your love for others when you've learned to love yourself. Yes, it's possible to admire others and desire to connect with them. However, you can't form a solid and healthy relationship with them if you haven't first accepted your uniqueness.

For any relationship to thrive in love, both parties must be able to build on their self-esteem; that is, the individuals involved must have a strong sense of self-worth so they can support each other.

Recognizing that you cannot give love to others if you don't have it within yourself helps you to grow in self-esteem, which stems from confidence. Just as you cannot pour from an empty cup, you need to find love for yourself so you can genuinely connect with others, be emotionally available for them and love them.

Building self-esteem involves healing from past wounds and overcoming the trials that may have affected your sense of self-worth, identity, perspective, and view on life. Many of us have experienced situations that have shaken our confidence and shattered our self-esteem. However, it is possible to recover from these scars and develop a healthy sense of self-love that comes from within rather than from our past negative experiences or external validation.

Having a healthy level of self-esteem enables you to set more authentic and meaningful goals for yourself. Oftentimes, we set goals based on pessimism. For instance, detesting your body structure, feeling ineffective at work, or like 'disappointment' in certain activities.

However, when we cultivate self-love, our perspective shifts. Instead of trying to 'fix' ourselves based on unrealistic standards, we learn to support ourselves. We gain a clearer understanding of our worth and abilities. And with this knowledge, we can set goals that align with our values and aspirations and that genuinely contribute to our personal growth.

In particular, you deserve the same level of esteem and respect that you so freely give to others. There is no need to justify or explain why you value yourself. You are praiseworthy, just as you are, and you can extend that honor to others.

Self-esteem encompasses having the same level of respect and consideration for yourself that you have for others, and it should be a fundamental principle in how you treat yourself and those around you. However, it's not always easy to practice self-esteem. Sometimes, we may find ourselves caught up in expectations or questioning our worth. While we desire self-esteem, we may struggle to embrace it fully. That's why we need confidence.

After examining the significance of confidence in building self-esteem and understanding its essence, it is important to be aware of the factors that can dampen self-esteem. Recognizing these obstacles is crucial to avoid building self-esteem, only to have it undermined. Here are three broad impediments to self-esteem:

1. When your internal pundit opposes everything, you do.

Your internal pundit is the voice in your head that judges, criticizes, and taunts everything you try to do. When the internal critic is strong, and you believe you are the cause of all your problems, it can hit you where it hurts the most. It reminds you of the mistakes you made while parenting or leading the group at work, and it lingers, refusing to let it go.

It may very well be challenging to handle the internal pundit, as it tends to feed on itself: you make a mistake, the internal critic talks to you about it, and you become upset, unable to let it go. Your mindset changes, your mood drops, you say something harsh or neglectful because you're feeling bad, and the internal critic grows stronger. This cycle continues as you become more stressed, amplifying the power of the internal critic. It creates a compounding phenomenon that can be difficult to break free from.

When you're unable to quiet your internal critic, it follows you wherever you go, from one place to another, event to event. It becomes a constant companion, casting its judgment and criticism on your every action and decision. It can feel like an unrelenting presence, impacting your self-esteem and overall well-being.

2. When you set very high standards for yourself.

There is a difference between having minimum expectations and having excessively high assumptions. Principles can be a device of confidence; "I won't endure being addressed discourteously," or "I anticipate that individuals in my day-to-day existence should regard my limits." Coming down on yourself to satisfy unimaginable guidelines is the flip side.

There is a difference between setting reasonable expectations and having excessively high assumptions. Having personal boundaries and principles can be a tool for developing confidence. For example, setting a boundary of not tolerating disrespect or expecting others to respect your boundaries. However, being overly harsh on yourself and setting unrealistic standards can hurt your self-esteem.

When you have highfalutin assumptions, you eventually end up unable to meet them. This can lead to feelings of disappointment or inadequacy. When your standards are over the top, you are more likely to 'fall short' and then punish yourself for not measuring up. It becomes difficult for you to go easy on yourself, and you struggle to be patient with yourself because you are disappointed at your inability to achieve that goal.

Giving yourself space to rest becomes a challenge when you feel you don't deserve it as you didn't accomplish your goals. When you devalue yourself in such a manner based on your shortcomings, it becomes hard to accept another opportunity to try again.

3. When it was not displayed for you.

Similarly to everything in life, building self-esteem is a skill that can be developed and mastered. Our early formative experiences have a significant impact on our self-esteem and confidence. I once read a definitive statement online and it said, "Be cautious with how you address your children; it turns into their internal voice.".

If you were spoken to with love and empathy as a child, you might have an easier time embracing love and developing self-esteem. But, if you grew up in an environment without kind voices or were raised by a reckless parent, it may be difficult for you to love yourself even as an adult.

The beauty of confidence is that when you cultivate it within yourself, you also develop a reservoir of compassion you can extend to those around you. There is nothing

EXTRACTING THE GOOD: THE IMPORTANCE OF SELF-LOVE

inherently wrong with you if you struggle with self-esteem; it is a common challenge that many adults face. But we can all learn to nurture and strengthen our confidence and self-esteem through education and practice. Just like any skill, it takes time and effort to cultivate self-esteem.

One of the remarkable aspects of cultivating confidence is that it helps you gain an understanding of why you may struggle with it and recognize the origin of those struggles. By reflecting on your past experiences and habits, you already begin to put in the work of developing self-awareness and empathy. This introspection allows you to show compassion for yourself, which is a vital component of genuine self-love.

When you recognize your desire to show yourself more love, you defeat the snags that stand in your path. When you harness these tools which are at your disposal, you can work towards cultivating self-love and start to approach life from a place of confidence. Your thoughts shape your actions, and your actions shape your behavior. As you consistently embody self-love in your behavior, it helps set a standard for you and those around you.

The aforementioned are the factors that can dampen one's

self-esteem. However, it's not a lost cause. If you would want to grow in confidence, you can use these 3 tips to boost and maintain your self-esteem.

1. *Talk to yourself the way you'd talk to someone you love.*

Reflect on what you tell yourself when you're disappointed, upset, or humiliated. Imagine redirecting the same emotions toward your friend, partner, or relative. Visualize them sitting across from you, expressing those negative thoughts and feelings about themselves. How would you respond in such a situation?

Dr. David discusses a helpful technique called "the twofold norm" in his book, "The Inclination Great Handbook." He suggests that you can imagine someone you love expressing the same negative self-talk you're experiencing. Picture them saying those things to you and note how you would respond to them.

This is an excellent tool as it operates on multiple levels. Firstly, it silences the negative thoughts when you imagine using such harsh or unreasonable words on a loved one.

Can I speak to a friend in this manner? No. Would I be comfortable listening to my friends talk about themselves in this way? No. Your answer to these questions helps create a contrast between how you treat others and yourself.

As discussed earlier, negative self-talk can quickly spiral and become overwhelming. But if you prevent it from escalating in the first place, you can gain control over it. Even if you don't have ample time to engage in a detailed conversation and analyze what you would say to a friend going through the same situation, simply interrupting your negative thought process is a significant step.

At this point, the next level of this tool comes into play. It involves unpacking the thoughts and responding with kindness. Even if you don't have the immediate opportunity or energy to reflect on the episode fully, you can revisit it at a later time when you're in a safe space.

2. *Take care of yourself.*

Taking care of yourself or paying attention to your needs once in a blue moon doesn't automatically turn you into a self-love coach. Engaging in daily acts of self-care can shape your mindset, just like consistent actions form our behaviors, habits, and character in general.

Also, self-care is not limited to going for a 'spa day.' Self-care is addressing your needs, whether physical or personal. It allows you to show up as your best self in the world. Just like you can't pour from an empty cup, you need to prioritize refilling your cup. If you're empty, you have nothing to offer to yourself and those around you.

While it is true that a trip to the spa is the best form of self-care for some people, there are many other ways to lay back and give yourself a special moment. You could reach out to a friend or loved one and strike up meaningful conversations or meditate. Reschedule and give yourself time to rest, take a walk in the park, watch a YouTube video on how to make a quilt, or learn how to cook your favorite meal – any of these can also be a form of self-care.

You can create a list of self-care activities you enjoy and work towards checking off each item on your list!

See a movie. Drink water. Make a list of the things you are grateful for. Take an exquisite bubble bath and light as many candles as possible. Tune in to your favorite digital broadcast or podcast.

The possibilities are endless, and finding out what works for you matters.

3. Set boundaries

One of the most empowering ways to build your confidence is by developing the ability to self-advocate. You demonstrate self-care and worth by standing up for yourself and expressing your needs. Setting boundaries for yourself and others is a powerful means of communicating and taking a stab at your needs.

Setting boundaries starts with acknowledging and affirming what they are. The process of identifying your boundaries is rooted in recognizing your self-worth and the validation you give yourself. Taking the time and effort to uphold our boundaries is a continuous act of self-care. When you establish limits, you can define your values and clarify your objectives. You gain a deeper understanding of what is important to you, learn how to carry yourself, and acknowledge that it is perfectly valid to be discerning about your intentions and priorities.

When you effectively communicate your boundaries to others, you attract people who respect those boundaries, creating an environment of mutual regard you can consistently uphold. Boundaries form a type of protection; when you establish and enforce boundaries, you safeguard yourself. Think about the people in your life whom you feel compelled to protect. You understand that part of the reason you go to great lengths to protect them is that you love them. Similarly, you express self-love when you protect yourself by enforcing healthy boundaries.

Personal Space and Relationship: An Individual Brain Research Idea

When actively using these confidence tools to enhance self-esteem, it's important to remember that communicating your boundaries to others can sometimes evoke strong emotions—in such moments, reminding yourself that "affection" and "like" are two distinct concepts is helpful. For example, you may always love your best friend, even if there are times when you may not appreciate their behavior or feel unavailability.

Much like any relationship, self-esteem can present challenges and requires effort to cultivate and maintain. It can sometimes feel like a test, or to a large extent, like a battle to feel affection by all means. However, just as you recognize the underlying love in your friendships, it's important to remind yourself that the same love exists within you, even when you feel like it's dwindled. Be kind and patient with yourself, and guard your self-esteem

EXTRACTING THE GOOD: THE IMPORTANCE OF SELF-LOVE

meticulously.

Over the last few years, circumstances have led most of us to invest more energy and spend more time with ourselves. Whether you became distant from everyone during the lockdown or worked in a much more confined space, the truth is that we have been less 'occupied' socially. During this time, we experienced fewer external distractions and a significant reduction in the need to seek approval and validation from others. It has provided an opportunity for us to delve deeper into our thoughts, emotions, and values.

Confidence doesn't mean that you are entirely content with being alone; rather, it enables you to find inner peace and accept your individuality. The past two years have shown us that our most constant companion throughout our lives is ourselves and being in touch with our Creator. Our thoughts and sentiments about ourselves may not be as cheerful; however, the importance of confidence, self-esteem, and self-worth cannot be overemphasized.

EXTRACTING THE GOOD: THE IMPORTANCE OF SELF-LOVE

NOTES TO SELF

CHAPTER 6

DIVINE CREATIVITY

When you think of "creativity," what comes to mind? Creativity can manifest in various forms, bringing forth a multitude of ideas and inspiring change in the world. However, creativity is also a complex concept due to the multitude of outlets available, presenting two things: a test and an open door. For instance, it is easy to attend work meetings without recognizing whose goals are genuine. Similarly, it is even easier to lose sight of your own goals.

Taking time to reflect on your personal qualities is an opportunity to help you identify which are being engaged creatively, considering the many facets of your traits. This perspective can provide insights into what truly constitutes a creative attribute, helping you determine whether you recognize or overlook your "creative" side. It may seem like a demanding task, but it can offer valuable insights into your creative journey.

At times, you need to focus on yourself; other times, you

need to focus on your purpose and understand what true creativity entails. Creativity stands out; it defies specific definitions and manifests in several ways. So, what are the attributes of a creative person? And do you possess any of them? Here are ten traits that can provide some insights.

Vivacious

Creative individuals possess a distinct energy that surrounds them. They exude vibrant and passionate energy, putting their whole heart into whatever they devote their time and energy to. This sort of energy is unique, different from mere hyperactivity, and it propels them in a positive direction and is not erratically expended.

The energy fuels them to pour their passion into their art and share that energy with others who see what they've made. The infectious nature of their enthusiasm allows them to uplift and inspire others. Trust me, this energy is unlike anything else, and if you have experienced it before, you'll know exactly what I mean.

Clever

Another trait creative individuals possess is cleverness. Creative individuals possess a variety of shrewdness in their minds, like a hidden talent waiting to be unleashed.

They are savvy and use this skill to connect with their environment. Intelligence can take various forms, but creative individuals often excel in the realm of abstract and imaginative thinking.

Discernment is another significant aspect of their mental prowess because with increased knowledge comes greater creative achievements.

Delicate

While being insightful is a predominant trademark, creative individuals also possess a sensitive side. They are delicate to numerous things because their hearts are continually open to the world. They are very sensitive and emotional.

Creatives also can perceive both the delight and agony of everyday life, making them susceptible to the entire spectrum of human experience. This sensitivity and vulnerability allow them to shed any self-doubt and put their all into their work. While a delicate heart may be seen as vulnerable, it is truly a gift for creative individuals.

Aggressive

Creatives are aggressive about their interests. They are constantly searching for the next task and have an insatiable thirst for new experiences. Nothing can deter their desire to have a go at something novel and unconventional.

Their continuous action is like fuel that drives their quest for more. They are always on the lookout for inspiration, drawing from the smallest moments in their day to the most significant events in their lives. They find meaning and motivation in every experience, using them as motivation for their creative work.

Gullible

Another characteristic that is often found in creative individuals is a sense of naivety. While being naive and gullible can be seen as risky in this world, creative people often find themselves falling into that guileless pool.

However, being gullible is not necessarily dangerous; it

can help creatives grow and learn from their mistakes. It can unintentionally open doors and lead to more mind-blowing discoveries. There is a certain amount of innocence in creative individuals as they look at the world with hopeful eyes and try to see the best in humanity. Being curious or having a meandering spirit remains inseparable from being guileless.

As a creative, the world is your playground, but you must also be cautious, as sometimes the world can bite back.

Defiant

Creatives are indeed remarkably defiant. They face heaps of challenges frequently and will not hesitate to wreck, knowing that even in failure, there may be valuable lessons and positive outcomes.

They may bear the scars of their mistakes and setbacks with pride, but their defiance keeps their heart and passion burning. With a heart brimming with fire and a resilient spirit, creatives are impervious to the harshest criticism from others. Their defiance propels them to think outside the box and explore uncharted territories, even if it means facing potential disappointment. They choose to see every experience as an opportunity for growth, regardless of the outcome.

Outgoing and Independent

Can one individual at any point be both extroverted and introverted? Creatives sure can! They have different sides to them, the side they show to the public and the private side. A creative person can be sociable and independent, talkative and quiet, shy and confident within one body.

Creatives can often embrace both their extroverted and introverted sides with distinct advantages. They appreciate the benefits of being outgoing and engaging with others and the advantages of solitude.

Energetic

Creatives thrive on being lively; their presence most times lights up the room. They approach their work with a sense of joy and experimentation, continuously exploring and pushing boundaries until they achieve their desired outcome.

They play with colors to find the perfect hue, experiment with different angles to capture the ideal photograph and manipulate materials to create the perfect sculpture, and you know very well that creatives tend to be reckless. They understand that being energetic allows them to infuse their work with a sense of fun, turning seemingly hard tasks into pure delight. It encourages them to take risks, embrace serendipity, and discover unexpected beauty and breakthroughs. Most times, by being carefree, creatives find inspiration and create their best work, often stumbling upon brilliance in the most unexpected and fascinating ways.

Liberal

If there's anyone who epitomizes openness, it's your creative friend or anybody immersed in the world of creativity. Being liberal is a significant trait, considering how receptive creatives need to be to achieve success.

Being open-minded enables creatives to climb mountains and venture into unexplored terrains. It allows them to view things and situations from different standpoints. while avoiding the confines of limits or restrictions. Being liberal allows creatives to be free and explore their thoughts, the sky being their breaking point.

Visionary

Creatives are perpetual dreamers. Their minds are filled with dreams and aspirations, during the day, at night, in the evening, and once more the following day. These dreams stem from their deep sense of purpose and desire to achieve their goals.

While creatives may occasionally indulge in fantasies, like any individual, their dreams are often grounded in reality. When an idea captures the imagination of a creative, they pursue it wholeheartedly, even if it initially starts as a mere dream.

Do you recognize any of these qualities within yourself? These are just a few examples of the many traits that creative individuals possess. However, even if you don't currently exhibit these traits, it doesn't mean you're not creative or incapable of developing them over time. Some of these qualities may come naturally to you, while others can be learned and nurtured. Whether you find a few or all of these characteristics within you, embrace them and unleash your creative potential. Remember, creativity resides within each of us, and tapping into it adds vibrance to our lives. So, don't hesitate to channel your inner creativity and let it thrive.

ability
IS WHAT YOU'RE CAPABLE OF DOING.

motivation
DETERMINES WHAT YOU WILL DO.

attitude
DETERMINES HOW WELL YOU DO IT.

NOTES TO SELF

CHAPTER 7

BRINGING BALANCE

Life is often like a complex exercise as we navigate precarious situations and continually shuffle between work, home, finances, health, and relationships.

In our pursuit of success and reaching our goals, it becomes crucial to recognize the significance of maintaining balance in our lives. Balancing these different aspects allows us to lead a more fulfilling life with fewer regrets.

Keeping an even life isn't only vital for your well-being, satisfaction, and prosperity but also fundamental for supporting efficiency, overseeing pressure, and releasing your potential.

Striving for a balanced life is vital for your well-being, satisfaction, and prosperity and fundamental for fostering productivity, managing stress, and unlocking your full potential.

How do you aim to accomplish balance? You can follow these five practical ways to attain balance.

1. *Take some time off*

Take some time to get rest to help ease your mind. Unwind and recharge. You can do so by dedicating a few hours each day or during the weekend to retreat. Switch off your workstations and mobile phones, and fully engage in activities that promote relaxation. You can read a book, practice meditation, go for a walk, or engage in a meaningful conversation with a friend or relative. I understand the temptation to check your notifications or social media updates, but it's important to remind yourself that these things can wait.

Establish boundaries between work and rest. Avoid the temptation to let work invade your time. It'll only increase stress and hamper your productivity, negatively impacting your relationships. Once you're done with work for the day, make a conscious effort to shift your focus away from work-related matters.

2. *Embrace a solid way of life*

The quality of your well-being influences every aspect of your life. Therefore, investing in your physical and mental health is crucial. Adopt healthy habits, get adequate rest, stay hydrated, and engage in regular exercise.

3. *Keep away from cynicism*

Maintaining a positive mindset and minimizing negative influences is essential for safeguarding your inner peace and happiness. Distance yourself from toxic people as much as possible. Cultivate gratitude, refrain from self-criticism ,and make it a point to engage in at least one activity each day that brings you joy.

4. *Figure out how to focus on*

Creating balance is not about cramming as many things as possible into your daily life. It involves assessing what is truly important (and what is not) and determining how much time and resources you should invest in the things that make a difference to you.

Is it necessary to respond to that work email during a family evening gathering? Is buying that expensive purse more important than saving money for a down payment on your dream home? Regularly assess your priorities to stay on track, manage your time effectively, and prevent burnout.

5. Spoil yourself

Taking time to indulge yourself can improve your mood, emotional well-being, and confidence. Set aside some time for yourself occasionally. Plan a spa visit, go out of town for shopping, or dine at your favorite café. And if you want to relax without breaking the bank, try listening to music, taking a relaxing bath, or simply staying in bed.

Start integrating these practices into your daily life and see the difference.

The Significance of a Healthy Lifestyle

Maintaining a healthy lifestyle is increasingly important for your well-being and success in today's fast-paced world. A balanced diet and regular physical fitness can greatly enhance and stabilize your overall health and well-being.

Figuring out the significance of a healthy lifestyle.

❖ How would a balanced, healthy lifestyle affect you?

We live in a world with diverse prevailing beliefs and opinions, so it's natural for one person's response to a question to differ from another's. The internet, especially social media, provides access to a wide range of information on exercise and nutrition. Every day, we see 'fresh out of the box new' diets being advertised, each claiming to be the latest standard. From low-carb and high-fat diets to low-glycemic load (GL), macrobiotics, carb cycling, gluten/grain-free, Thinning World, or Herbalife, our minds are constantly exposed to conflicting information.

It's important to note the key aspects associated with a balanced lifestyle. Fortunately, there are many reliable online sources available to assist you in maintaining this balance. The National Health Service (NHS), for instance, offers a wealth of information through its 'Live Well' section, which covers a wide range of topics, including healthy meals and getting started with fitness.

The minefield of conflicting information extends beyond just dieting; it can also be confusing to find a definitive answer on the best types of exercise for achieving a well-balanced lifestyle. Numerous sources are advocating for different workouts, from weightlifting and high-intensity interval training (HIIT) to marathon running, yoga, CrossFit, or circuit training. Engaging in any form of physical activity contributes to maintaining this balance. If you discover a sport or training program that you enjoy, it's beneficial to stick with it. Consistency is key, as it greatly impacts your overall well-being and balance in life.

❖ What direction is the most effective way to keep a healthy lifestyle?

No definitive answer applies to everyone, regardless of what you might be asking. Each person's body and mind respond differently, and finding the right balance is a personal journey.

It is necessary to find the balance that brings you joy. It's too easy to feel like you're doing everything wrong, especially when you are constantly comparing yourself to people on social media who seem to have made it on and achieved the perfect life. However, the issue here is not to be hard on yourself; everyone has their path. Living a healthy life doesn't happen suddenly, it is the accumulation of all the positive changes and decisions you make along the way. If you veer off course and take a wrong turn, it's not a catastrophe; you need to keep going—it's all part of the journey. Keep it simple and be compassionate towards yourself.

Key Approaches to Foster a Balanced Lifestyle

Everybody unexpectedly answers to exercise and diet; notwithstanding, there are various steps you can take to maintain a well-balanced life.

- Be Careful and Care For Yourself

To achieve a healthy lifestyle, ensure you are taking care of yourself. Your body requires adequate rest, regular exercise, and nutritious food. Set aside time in your busy day to engage in activities that can help you relax, such as reading or practicing meditation.

- Be Coordinated

Planning and coordination are essential for maintaining a balanced mindset. It allows you to allocate time for your responsibilities while making room for other activities. Staying organized helps to resist stress and enhance your overall life balance.

- Define Your Objectives

Achieving your objectives can contribute to fostering a positive outlook. Your objectives can cover anything from your work, finances, or wellness.

- Eat Properly

Your body needs good food varieties and supplements to make new cells, clean poisons, and function appropriately. Guaranteeing you get your 5 dailies can assist with working on your eating regimen and life balance. Consider fasting regularly. Eating one meal a day has significant advantages and allows the body to properly digest foods, according to the book, *How to Eat to Live* by Elijah Muhammad.

Primary Advantages of Maintaining a Balanced Lifestyle

Ensuring a balanced lifestyle offers a multitude of evident reasons. Here are some key benefits that come with maintaining a healthy life balance.

- Decreases pressure
- Works on overall well-being and prosperity
- Works on your psychological perspective; helpguide.org recommends eating properly and maintaining a balance as an effective tool against discouragement.
- Assists with supporting your energy - Eating well provides your body with the necessary nutrients and with energy
- Works on your temperament - balance improves your state of mind; healthy habits and positive relationships can keep the brain working optimally.

Gratitude: A Powerful Tool for Enhancing Well-being

Gratitude is a fundamental tool we have at our disposal to improve our well-being and positively impact others. It can remarkably transform the negativities around us into positivities, turns denial into acceptance, chaos into order, and confusion into clarity. It allows us to embrace our past, find peace in the present and create a vision for the future.

From a young age, we are taught to express gratitude when someone gives us a gift or extends a kind gesture. It becomes an automatic response, ingrained as a social norm. However, how often do we extend gratitude for the small, positive things that occur in our daily lives? Do we truly recognize the abundance for which we can be grateful?

We have come across various meanings of gratitude through hearing and reading, but truly experiencing the essence of gratitude requires a conscious effort. How often do we utter the words "thank you" without taking a moment to genuinely feel grateful?

Genuine gratitude goes beyond surface expressions and involves a deep, heartfelt appreciation for the things we receive, tangible or intangible. It is a conscious and positive emotion we express which requires us to pause, reflect, and truly feel the impact of what we are grateful for. Practicing gratitude entails recognizing the gestures of others towards us or the things that are going well in our lives. It involves a process of acknowledging the positive aspects of life and their impact.

Regularly expressing gratitude brings about numerous benefits, both in the short and long term. Analysts have extensively studied gratitude and consider it a cornerstone of positive psychology. Evidence suggests that individuals who intentionally acknowledge the good things in their lives tend to experience greater happiness and lower levels of depression. But how does this happen?

1. Being Appreciative Changes your Mindset

    Research has shown that individuals who regularly practice gratitude exhibit increased brain activity in the medial prefrontal cortex, an area associated with learning and decision-making. This heightened brain activity suggests that gratitude positively impacts cognitive processes.

    Interestingly, the effects of gratitude extend beyond the immediate moment of expressing thanks. Studies have also found that the increased brain activity in the medial prefrontal cortex can persist for up to a month after the gratitude practice. This suggests that the benefits of gratitude can have lasting effects on the brain.

2. Being Thankful Can Overcome Feelings of Gloom

Expressing has a remarkable ability to elevate positive emotions, such as happiness and empathy, and redirect our focus toward the good in life. By consciously acknowledging and appreciating the positive aspects of our lives, we shift our attention away from toxic emotions like resentment and jealousy.

3. Gratitude Yields Long-term Benefits

Continuous acts of gratitude have a cumulative effect on your mindset and behavior, intensifying over time.

4. Gratitude Helps to Combat Grief

A study revealed that a single mindful act of gratitude leads to an immediate 10% increase in happiness and a 35% reduction in depressive symptoms. When gratitude becomes a habit, it can help prevent anxiety and depression. It also serves as a potent catalyst for happiness, igniting a flame of euphoria in your spirit.

5. Gratitude Improves Our Overall Wellbeing

In addition to reducing and counteracting negative emotions, gratitude is associated with other healthy behaviors, such as exercise. Research has also linked gratitude to stronger immune systems, reduced pain, lower blood pressure, and deeper, more refreshing sleep.

6. Gratitude Encourages Deeper Connections and Relationships

By cultivating gratitude, we enhance our capacity for forgiveness, become more inclined to help others, and develop empathy. Expressing gratitude can also contribute to greater satisfaction and fulfillment among colleagues, reducing the probability of burnout.

7. Expressing Gratitude Prompts Positive Activities

By expressing gratitude and nurturing our motivation to help others, a grateful mindset increases the likelihood of spreading the goodwill and happiness we experience. Research shows that gratitude may also motivate individuals to engage in positive behaviors and foster personal growth.

This has a positive impact on us on two levels. Firstly, when we adopt a grateful mindset, we tend to engage in various activities that enhance our well-being, such as meditation, physical exercise, and acknowledging our resources. Secondly, it cultivates kindness, empathy, and generosity within us.

Similarly, research conducted by Frederickson has demonstrated that when gratitude is expressed, it increases the likelihood of the recipient extending a favor to a third party, effectively expanding a network of goodwill.

The Two Phases of Gratitude

We have explored the benefits of gratitude and the importance of making it an active practice. While it may seem perfect, we understand that expressing gratitude can feel less natural in our busy lives or during times of stress.

To cultivate this mindset, it can be helpful to break it down into two steps: recognizing the goodness and identifying its source. Only then can we pinpoint specific actions to incorporate gratitude into our daily routines.

- Recognizing the good in our lives, at any point, even when things are not perfect

  The brain naturally tends to focus on what needs improvement, which is essential for survival and problem-solving. However, it is also important to cultivate the habit of recognizing and appreciating what is going well in our lives. By gaining perspective and allowing ourselves to rest and enjoy the positive aspects, we can experience a sense of joy and gratitude. Through this practice, we come to appreciate the many facets that make life worth living and recognize our role in creating and choosing them.

- Recognizing the wellsprings of goodness beyond yourself

Once we have acknowledged the beauty in our present circumstances, we can embark on the second phase of gratitude, recognizing the goodness that originates from the world outside ourselves. As we embrace this joy and appreciation, we reach a point where recognizing and expressing gratitude towards the people around us, nature, the Creator, or even our fortune becomes an integral and instinctive second step.

Appreciation allows us to recognize our connection to the rest of humanity and acknowledge the roles others play. This practice fosters stronger bonds among partners, families, friends, and colleagues, as it leads us to actively accept our interdependence, regardless of whether it prompts specific action.

The Five Methods for Expressing Gratitude

EXTRACTING THE GOOD: THE IMPORTANCE OF SELF-LOVE

Like any skill, you can learn and grow in the art of expressing gratitude. Here are some tips on how to continually express appreciation:

→ Take a moment to reflect on three things you are grateful for every day.

Cultivate the habit of recognizing the positive aspects of your life. This simple practice can have a direct impact on your mindset throughout the day and even improve the quality of your sleep. Therapists often recommend this practice as an important step in combating depression. To make it more effective, set aside ten minutes for this exercise instead of rushing through it. Writing down your gratitude list can be a powerful way to solidify your practice, and revisiting it at the end of the week can be beneficial.

→ Begin an appreciation journal.

Journaling can be a powerful self-care practice. When you write, you engage different parts of your brain and gain new perspectives on your memories and emotions. An appreciation journal has been shown to activate brain regions associated with morality and positive emotions. People who can find meaning and feel grateful for the good things that emerge from challenging situations demonstrate higher resilience, forgiveness, and resilience. Also, reading about what you are grateful for uplifts your spirit when you're struggling to stay positive.

→ Show gratitude to someone else every day

There are numerous individuals around us, and we are connected in various ways. How often do we carve out time to appreciate them more intentionally or thoughtfully? Sure, we say thank you every time the cashier at our local store hands us our purchase, or we thank our partner for setting the table, but do we take the time to make it meaningful?

Challenge yourself and choose someone new each week and find unique ways to express your gratitude. This could involve adopting more conscious non-verbal communication, such as maintaining eye contact, offering a genuine smile, and writing a heartfelt message acknowledging the positive influence of someone's actions on you. You could also express gratitude through a thoughtful gift or service gesture, maybe a shoulder massage. Be creative!

→ Ponder

Appreciation can be enhanced through the act of meditation. Engaging in guided meditations focused on love and compassion can expand our perspective on life and our connection with ourselves and others. It cultivates acceptance, forgiveness, and, ultimately, gratitude. During these moments of meditation, we can take the opportunity to visualize and immerse ourselves in the experiences or things we appreciate, allowing the feelings of gratitude to grow and deepen.

- Focus on the intentions of others

    When you receive a gift or a kind gesture from someone, take a moment to contemplate how they intend to bring positivity into your life. Reflect on their willingness to support you, bring joy to your emotions, or be there for you during a challenging moment. By acknowledging and appreciating their intentions, you better understand their thoughtfulness and enhance your gratitude for their actions.

Final Note on Gratitude

The art of gratitude is undoubtedly a powerful practice to develop. The goal is to make it a habit that becomes an integral part of our lives. It's important to remember that practice and persistence are essential in nurturing our intentions and aspirations. Start your journey of cultivating the art of gratitude today. With dedication and patience, you can make it a meaningful and fulfilling part of your life.

NOTES TO SELF

CHAPTER 8

STRENGTHENING RELATIONSHIPS

Humans are social creatures, and our well-being is often tied to the quality of our relationships. Whether we are introverts or extroverts, we all have a circle of family, friends, and acquaintances we interact with on a regular basis. Building and nurturing these connections is crucial for our overall happiness and personal growth.

Here are some insightful tips that can help you enhance your social skills and cultivate better relationships in your life.

→ Recognize the sentiments and necessities of others

   Engaging in your immediate social sphere can be effortless, but it's important to remember that effective communication goes beyond just expressing your thoughts and opinions. Building strong and lasting relationships requires that you create space for others to share their ideas and feelings. Listen actively and respect their right to hold onto their own opinions, even if they differ from yours.

→ Be open to ideas and making compromises

Making the best decision and choosing a course of action that benefits everyone involves soliciting input from all parties involved. Strive for a democratic approach when deciding where to go for dinner or dividing tasks among your friends. Understand that compromise will often be necessary. This may entail forfeiting certain preferences to accommodate the preferences of others.

→ Concentrate on the gig

Taking care of your business in the best way possible goes beyond merely working on the connection between you and your partners. It also implies reducing stress and cultivating inner peace during your leisure time. Doing so will make you less irritable and more vibrant when spending time with your friends, family, and loved ones.

→ Invest more of your free time with others rather than alone

Devoting quality time to your family, friends, partner, and colleagues is essential for developing deeper connections. It also provides an opportunity to relax and exchange various information. Spending more time outdoors with others can significantly improve your mental well-being by allowing you to discuss any issues you may have with your partner or friends. Addressing these issues prevents them from festering and straining your relationships.

→ Learn to control your feelings through regular practice

To prevent a conversation from growing into contention and to manage the intense emotions of others, you should be able to maintain emotional composure. This involves exercising control over your own emotions. Engaging in activities like Bikram yoga provides physical health benefits and helps you cultivate a calm and focused mindset. Additionally, taking a leisurely walk or going for a run can help clear your mind and release pent-up frustrations.

→ Work on your insecurities

Starting a conversation with a heavy burden of weaknesses can create a sense of anxiety and make it difficult for you to open up or connect with new people.

To address this, dedicate time each day to work on enhancing your appearance and adjusting your lifestyle choices to begin making small but meaningful improvements. It will also significantly improve your self-confidence and how you interact with others.

→ Familiarize yourself with the individual triggers of the people around you and try not to set them off

Just as you have your fears and vulnerabilities, everyone else does too. Certain topics and even specific words can trigger intense emotional responses in some individuals. So, when you become acquainted with someone, make an effort to identify these sensitive subjects and avoid triggering them during your interactions. They will appreciate your sensitivity and consideration, and it will help foster healthier relationships, even during challenging times.

→ Lighthearted banter is fine, but maintaining a positive tone

Consistently being critical and mocking others may not set off any major trigger, but it can gradually tarnish your image. It's important to create an environment where people enjoy conversing with you, so make sure to engage in pleasant conversations, offer positive remarks, and only dole out what they can handle.

- Apologize more often

    Let's be real for a moment. We all make mistakes and occasionally end up upsetting a friend, family member, or partner. It's critical to acknowledge your fault and genuinely apologize. A simple sentence like "I'm sorry" can go a long way in maintaining good relationships and repairing ones that have been strained.

- Learn to forgive

    This aspect goes hand in hand with rendering apologies. You can't continue to seek forgiveness from others while holding onto grudges and dwelling on negative feelings. While it's understandable that you might need some time to cool off, it's important to allow people to apologize so that you can move forward. If someone extends an olive branch, don't push them away.

- Free yourself from the emotional burden

    This point builds upon the previous one. Sometimes, people won't approach you for reconciliation or even acknowledge their wrongs. While you don't have to go to great lengths to mend broken friendships and relationships, it's important to release the burden of carrying resentment, allow your wounds to heal, and move forward without constantly being angry and blaming others for all your troubles.

- Spur solid conversations rather than stir up quarrels

Challenging issues will often arise, and addressing them with your life partner, friends, and colleagues is important. While sometimes, conflicts can be normal, engaging in a shouting match where everyone feels embarrassed will only drain you. Instead, strive to maintain composure. This is where the practice of mindfulness and deep breathing comes into play. Discuss your issues calmly, without raising your voice or interrupting one another, allowing for open and respectful communication.

- Quit worrying over little things.

Don't let minor issues escalate to the point of needing a conversation or resolution. Let it go if it is a trivial matter and don't dwell on it. While it might bother you temporarily, holding onto it will only lead to prolonged arguments and wasted time. It's better to prioritize harmony and let go of insignificant issues that have little impact on the bigger picture.

→ Quit overthinking things

Assume positive intentions in people's words and actions. Not everything someone says is meant as an insult or a veiled attack against you. People may not always have underlying meanings or malicious intentions behind their words. Quieten that negative inner voice and trust in the absence of clear evidence. This will help you remain calm and attentive and avoid unnecessary misunderstandings and conflicts over trivial matters.

→ Don't be in haste to make judgments or conclusions

While it's natural to be cautious and skeptical, it's important to avoid forming crazy speculations and creating scenarios in your mind that only fuel anger and resentment towards others. Don't let envy, anger, or insecurities cloud your judgment. Instead, focus on fostering open and effective communication that builds trust and understanding. Give others the benefit of the doubt and approach situations with a balanced and rational mindset.

→ Engage in active listening and ask thoughtful questions

Instead of immediately expressing your own opinions or demanding answers, take the time to genuinely listen to others and understand their perspective. This will help you stay away from issues.

Be attentive and make mental notes of important points they share. Then, after they have finished speaking, ask relevant questions to deepen the conversation further and demonstrate your interest in their thoughts and experiences. This approach helps to build mutual understanding and fosters meaningful connections between individuals.

→ Make analysis helpful

Adopting a constructive approach rather than resorting to criticism is better when providing feedback on someone's performance. Don't only point out their flaws; offer suggestions for improving and reaching the next level. Frame your feedback in a way that highlights areas for growth and development. Incorporate genuine compliments and acknowledge their strengths; this can help soften the impact of the critique. In the context of relationships, expressing gratitude for what your partner does well can motivate them to continue practicing and improving.

→ Prioritize spending time with your family regularly

Despite various responsibilities and commitments, it is important to make dedicated time for your parents, siblings, extended family, partner, and children. Set aside quality hours each week for immediate family interactions, and aim for monthly gatherings with extended family members. You can also stay connected through phone calls and conversations that help maintain the bond even when you're not physically together.

→ For significant relationships, pick your fights and let your partner win every once in a while.

Regardless of your relationship status, if you're committed to the long-term success of your relationship, you'll understand that there will be moments when you may end up on the losing side. Swallowing your pride, gracefully accepting defeat in an argument, and apologizing for any hurtful behavior, even if you believe you were technically right, are sacrifices to make to bury the hatchet.

One person in the relationship may find themselves doing this more frequently than the other, while the other person only does it occasionally. However, as long as it's for the small things and you both feel happy generally, it doesn't make any difference.

→ Your friend or partner will assume most of the responsibilities in a particular region, and that is okay

When it comes to household tasks such as keeping the house clean, meal planning, grocery shopping, or fixing things around the home, it's natural for one partner or spouse to excel or have a greater inclination towards certain tasks.

It becomes evident over time which is more organized and tidier, is handy with repairs, or has skills in specific areas. Rather than trying to divide all the tasks equally, allowing each person to take on the majority of the work in the areas they are skilled at and comfortable with can be more effective. This approach plays to their strengths and avoids unnecessary friction or dissatisfaction. Recognizing and leveraging each other's natural abilities can create a more harmonious division of labor within the household.

→ Try to avoid bothering people, teaching, or giving them undesirable examples

Open and clear communication is important in any relationship. After all, we all know that 'communication is key.' If you need to get something done or if you are feeling disappointed about something, it's better to express your feelings than hoard them. Don't be bossy or demand that things be done exactly the way you would do them just because you're used to it. Instead, communicate your thoughts and feelings concisely and respectfully without resorting to aggression or hostility.

→ Never make rash choices or begin discussions when you are angry

Avoid going to bed angry with your partner, making important decisions when you're angry or in a bad mood, and initiating difficult conversations when emotions are running high. Following these guidelines can help prevent impulsive actions or hurtful words you may regret later. Instead, take the time to cool off, gather your thoughts, and approach the situation with a calmer and more rational mindset. Doing so increases the likelihood of finding resolutions and maintaining healthy relationships.

→ Travel more and experience different cultures

EXTRACTING THE GOOD: THE IMPORTANCE OF SELF-LOVE

Traveling with companions, your partner, or family can be a wonderful opportunity to relax, experience new cultures, and strengthen your relationships. It allows you to step away from your usual responsibilities and enjoy quality time together. During your travels, you may also discover new aspects about each other that you were previously unaware of. While it may require effort and patience, following these guidelines consistently can lead to gradual improvements and increased happiness in your life.

BE THE Energy YOU WANT TO Attract

NOTES TO SELF

CHAPTER 9

WISDOM THROUGH EXPERIENCES

Wisdom is not something you automatically possess, rather, you gain it through experience. It is a virtue you can develop if you have genuine curiosity and willingness to explore new things and reflect upon their experiences. You can become smarter by actively seeking personal growth, examining your knowledge, and questioning assumptions.

Acquiring Experience

Try out new things. It is almost impossible to gain wisdom and high levels of knowledge when you are always indoors, repeating the same routine every day. You get savvier when you put yourself out there and allow yourself to learn, make mistakes, and reflect on your lessons from the experience.

If you are naturally reserved, work on developing a curious mind and the willingness to break off from your comfort zone and engage in new experiences. Each time you try something new, you expose yourself to the potential of learning and gaining more wisdom.

Going to places you've never been before is an incredible way to gain valuable experience. It could be booking a trip to a new city or taking a road trip to a nearby town. Challenge yourself to do new things. Try eating at a café that is popular with the locals instead of going to your #1 chain. Whenever you have the opportunity, choose novelty and uniqueness over what is familiar.

Attempting new friendly exercises is an effective method for opening up your reality. If you will invest your energy in watching sports, get passes to see a play. If you're a complete bibliophile, you could pursue a climbing club or join a bowling crew.

Attempting new social activities is a powerful way to broaden your horizons. If you love making crafts, consider stepping away for a moment and getting tickets to a baseball game. If you're an avid reader, challenge yourself to step outside your comfort zone and join a line-dance group or a sewing club.

Step out of your usual range of familiarity. When you feel hesitant or fearful about trying something new, that's often a sign that it's exactly what you should pursue. By confronting and overcoming challenges, you emerge stronger and more resilient, equipped to handle fear and uncertainty in the future. As Eleanor Roosevelt said, "You gain strength, courage, and confidence by every experience in which you really stop to look fear in the face. You are able to say to yourself, 'I lived through this awfulness. I can take the next thing that comes along.'"

For instance, volunteer to give a speech if you're nervous about public speaking. If you find it challenging to express your emotions, discuss it with a friend or family member and let them know what you think about it. Also, reciprocate their attention and inquire about their well-being.

Engaging in conversations with individuals you want to

learn from. Seek out people from diverse backgrounds and with different perspectives from yours, and approach these conversations with an open mind. Instead of judging them based on your viewpoint, make an effort to understand their experiences. The more you are ready to actively listen to and sympathize with others, the smarter you'll be.

Share yourself with individuals you're in with, as well. Work on going deeper than superficial topics to foster meaningful friendships.

Tip: Cultivate the skill of being an attentive listener and engage in conversations by asking questions. Focus on the speaker and actively listen while resisting the urge to let your mind wander. Each interaction presents an opportunity to gain insights, broaden your horizons, and deepen your understanding of others. This, in turn, contributes to your growth in wisdom.

Be liberal. Instead of hastily judging things you barely know about, approach them from different viewpoints and try to understand them. It's natural to form our opinions based on the limited experiences we've had in life, but there are more effective ways to gain wisdom. While you can't control the circumstances of your upbringing or the people you've been exposed to, you can choose to be receptive to exploring different cultures and lifestyles.

Avoid basing your judgments on what others think or how popular the idea is. Take the time to examine and explore both sides of the story before forming your opinion on something.

For instance, let's say you believe a certain genre of music isn't cool because none of your friends like it. Instead of getting on board with that temporary fad, attend a live performance of a band playing that genre and find out about its history and influences. By making an effort to understand something, you can confidently decide whether you like it or not. Don't pass judgment prematurely. Allow yourself to gain a deeper understanding before drawing conclusions.

Gaining from Shrewd Individuals

Invest in your personal growth through education. If you're keen on acquiring new knowledge and skills, taking a class is an excellent way to achieve that. These classes can be affiliated with a university but don't have to be.

Explore whether your local community offers classes or workshops taught by experts in their respective fields. It could be a cooking class, art workshop, language course, or any other subject that piques your interest.

Independent learning is also as valuable as formal classes when it comes to acquiring knowledge. If you don't have access to a class on a topic you're interested in, there are other ways to learn. Explore books available at the library, conduct interviews with knowledgeable individuals, and engage in hands-on learning experiences.

For example, if you want to learn a new language, you can choose to take a class or do a personal study. Join language conversation groups to practice with native speakers, read books written in the language, and consider traveling to a country where the language is spoken to enhance your language skills.

Track down wise coaches. Who in your life strikes you as smart? Wisdom can manifest in various forms. It could be a minister who provides thought-provoking messages every week, an inspiring teacher who shares their knowledge with passion, or a family member who consistently approaches challenges with a clear and rational mindset.

Take the time to reflect on why you think this person is smart. Is it because he or she is well-read and knowledgeable? Does he or she consistently provide valuable advice and support when others are in need? Do their demeanor and actions suggest that they have a deep understanding of life?

What could you possibly gain from that person? What life choices and ways of conduct can serve as an example for you? They can serve as role models for you. Try asking yourself what they would do in challenging situations and draw inspiration from their wisdom and approach.

Read as much as possible. Reading allows you to scour different perspectives, regardless of the subject matter. It provides insights into the thoughts and feelings of others that may be difficult to obtain differently. Exploring various viewpoints on significant issues gives you the information necessary to form informed opinions and make thoughtful decisions.

Understand that everyone is fallible. As you gain wisdom and experience, you will realize that even those you once looked up to as mentors or guides have their flaws. Avoid placing individuals on pedestals and holding them to unattainable standards, as their slip-ups can often be shocking and off-putting. Endeavor to see the humanity in people, acknowledging that they have both strengths and weaknesses. Embrace a balanced perspective that allows you to recognize both the good and the bad in others.

Practice forgiveness when someone you admire makes a mistake – try to put yourself in their shoes rather than kicking them when they're down. It's important to recognize that every individual, including parents, is fallible and faces challenges in finding the right path, just like everyone else. Reaching a point where you see your folks as equals who make mistakes, just like everyone else, demonstrates growth and wisdom.

Incorporating Wisdom

Be humble in new situations. As Socrates famously said, "The only true wisdom is in knowing you know nothing." You'll understand this idea better when you encounter a challenging situation that defeats all you think you know. No matter how intelligent you are or how many experiences you've had, there will be times when the line between good and bad seems blurry, and you need help in making decisions.

Approach new situations with an open mind and avoid assuming that you have all the answers. Instead, take the time to examine the situation from different perspectives, reflect on it, and seek advice if needed. Follow the lead of your inner voice.

Recognize and accept your limitations; it is a sign of wisdom. Understand your strengths and weaknesses and make the most of your abilities without pretending to possess knowledge or skills that you don't have.

Think before you act. Evaluate the situation by weighing the pros and cons, taking into account both your own experiences and the recommendations of others. Try to make the best decision possible based on careful consideration.

Tip: Don't hesitate to seek help when you need it. Go to someone you consider wise and ask for their advice. However, consider the advice given by someone you trust in the context of your judgment. In the end, you have the final say in determining your course of action; you are the one responsible for your actions.

Align your actions with your values. While seeking guidance from others, religious principles, and books can provide valuable insights, it's also important to critically evaluate and select the values that truly resonate with you. Your values should agree with your conscience, that premonition that guides you in light of what you know to be right. When you are faced with critical decisions, rely on your values as a guiding compass and stay true to them.

For instance, suppose a situation arises at work where someone is being harassed, and you know that standing up for them might upset your supervisor. What's the best thing to do in such a case? Consider the situation carefully and determine what holds greater significance to you: keeping your job or supporting someone who is being harmed.

Stand firm in your values, even in the face of criticism. It can be challenging because, throughout life, people try to impose their beliefs on you. Separate your values from others and be bold to do what you know is right, regardless.

Learn from your mistakes. Avoid being too hard on yourself when you make an error. You're human; making mistakes is part of your journey and learning process. Try to embrace the lessons and insights that come from these experiences, no matter how bitter they may be.

Understand that perfection can't possibly exist. The goal is to be more heavenly and grow into a better version of yourself. So, make an effort to follow up on your inner voice and endeavor to be a decent individual throughout life.

Share your insight with others. Don't just dish out instructions; lead by example. Show others the wisdom in being open, nonjudgmental, and smart in every situation. Reflect on the mentors who have guided you along the way and find ways to play that role for others who could benefit from what you have learned.

When someone seeks advice, do your best to guide them in the right direction. Avoid letting your desires cloud your advice, and provide objective and thoughtful guidance based on your experiences and knowledge.

NOTES TO SELF

CHAPTER 10

DO IT FOR SELF (SELF-LOVE)

In a world that often emphasizes putting others first, prioritizing self-love can sometimes feel selfish. Being mindful of your self-worth can bring about feelings of guilt, causing us to struggle with practicing self-love. It can be frustrating because we understand the importance of self-love, yet we find it challenging to embrace it fully. It's a surprising paradox, isn't it?

We live in a time when the confidence transformation is picking up, but we often struggle to fully embrace it because it contradicts what we were taught and raised to believe. Self-love was not emphasized in our education, and many of us didn't learn about it in our homes either.

We were taught the importance of putting others first and achieving success. We learned to work hard and make money. However, we neglected to learn how to prioritize our well-being and maintain a sense of personal fulfillment along the way.

You are only confined by the Walls You Build YOURSELF

One of my favorite quotes by W.E.B. Du Bois states, "The most important thing to remember is this: to be ready at any moment to give up what you are for what you might become."

Self-love is the bedrock of our identity, providing us with the fuel we need to navigate through life. When this bedrock is strong, everything else falls into place, and we experience a sense of stability and confidence. Those of us who have tasted the power of self-love can attest to its transformative effects. Once we start embracing self-love, we witness positive shifts in our lives. We find that life flows more smoothly, and it becomes easier to handle challenges. Our relationships deepen, our well-being improves, and life starts to feel far better— incredibly great. Cherishing yourself first and cultivating a deep, inner relationship brings forth numerous benefits. When you embark on this journey of self-love, you will:

1. *Perceive + Focus on Your Requirements*

You'll need to recognize your needs to establish that caring relationship with yourself. Without self-love, you overlook your own needs while prioritizing the needs of others, such as your partners, friends, family, and colleagues. Self-love involves identifying your needs and prioritizing them daily. It's about doing what genuinely feels right for you.

2. *Acquire a Genuine Identity*

Say goodbye to codependency. Self-love empowers you to take care of your own needs. You will learn to provide for yourself, and in doing so, you will grow into the person you want to be. You will celebrate the beauty and freedom of being true to yourself and develop a solid sense of your identity. Self-love helps you establish your authentic self.

3. *Put down Cherishing Stopping points.*

As your self-esteem grows, so will your ability to discern what is and isn't good for you. The more you love yourself, the less you will tolerate being treated like garbage. You will gain the clarity needed to understand what you will no longer accept.

4. Forestall Self-destructive behavior

You know when everything is finally going perfectly, and then you ruin that great feeling suddenly by doing something awful? Self-love helps eliminate that saboteur behavior. As we cultivate love within ourselves, embracing good things in our lives becomes easier.

5. Drop the Casualty Attitude

Self-love is about taking ownership, accepting responsibility for your actions, and how you choose to appear in this world. The primary reason you play the victim is that you fail to recognize the role you play in your experiences. When you begin to prioritize self-love, you start to perceive your experiences differently. It becomes about learning lessons rather than denying them. Ownership is empowering.

6. Give Love Without Feeling Drained

Airline stewards advise you to wear your oxygen masks before helping others with theirs. Why? Because you can't assist others if you're not able to breathe. Self-love works similarly. You can't give love to others if you don't have that love within yourself. You might think you can love, but what's happening is you're giving love from an empty place, further depleting your energy and draining the resources you're struggling to maintain. This leads to feelings of exhaustion, emptiness, and burnout after constantly giving to others. However, when you prioritize self-love and replenish your reserves, you'll be giving love from a full tank. This kind of giving feels invigorating and fulfilling.

7. *View as Your Own Cheerful*

Stop searching for happiness outside of yourself. You won't find it. Yes, you may find fleeting moments of joy but won't find lasting happiness. Self-love helps you reclaim your positive energy. It's quite simple, really. The more love you show yourself, the better you feel. And the better you feel, the happier you become. You hold the key to your happiness, and self-esteem is the path to discovering it.

Self-love isn't selfish. It's about reconnecting with your core needs, embracing the freedom of being yourself, and honoring your true essence while letting go of negative patterns. Loving yourself is transformative — nurturing a profound relationship with yourself will significantly enhance every aspect of your life. So go ahead, release the guilt, and embrace the profound joy of cultivating a deep, loving relationship with yourself.

We all aspire to become the best version of ourselves, and it's natural to wonder if personal growth is possible once we reach adulthood. The answer is a resounding yes. There are proven methods for self-improvement that can help you enhance various aspects of your life. However, this answer may raise further questions and curiosity.

Having looked at the benefits that come with self-love, what is the best way to improve yourself from a personal standpoint? What approach is the simplest? And what are the key aspects of self-love to focus on?

Taking into account your success and the well-being of others, here are some fundamental ways to achieve personal growth:

→ *Curb Anger*

It can lead to increased stress and unexpected complications, complicating our lives and hindering our ability to be the best version of ourselves. That is why learning to manage and let go of anger is crucial for personal improvement.

Letting go of your anger is hardly an easy task. However, the first step is understanding your anger and knowing what to do when you experience it.

Recognizing anger is often essential, as it allows you to acknowledge when you feel upset and choose to address this emotion rather than denying it or lashing out at others as a coping mechanism. Focus on being aware of when you feel angry and why, and understand that there is a distinction between feeling anger and acting on that anger. Then, explore your options for effectively managing and expressing your anger in healthy ways.

You can decide to change your convictions concerning things that anger you. You can do this by getting more familiar with the situation or reminding yourself that there may be things you don't know.

You can tell yourself that perhaps the person who cut you off in traffic was distracted by something challenging in their own life. If a friend seems rude to you, inquire about how their day is going to see if there is more to the situation that you are unaware of. These practices can reduce tension for you and ease feelings of anger.

You can also pay attention to your "anger triggers" and eliminate them when possible. For example, if you find yourself getting frustrated and angry when you're rushed, work on creating more space in your schedule (even if it means saying "no" a bit more), and try to remove that trigger. If a particular person drives you mad, consider limiting their role and appearance in your life if it doesn't involve resolving issues through communication with them first.

It's also important to learn how to let go of grudges and lingering resentment daily. Don't wake up holding onto resentment from the previous night when there's something you can do about it. Focus on forgiveness, even if it means not allowing someone who has wronged you to continue playing a significant role in your life. This becomes easier when you stay in the present as much as possible.

Practicing stress relievers like meditation can also help you let go of anger. Concentrate on releasing the grip that the past may have on you. Redirect your attention to the present moment, and it becomes easier to avoid rumination and stay in a positive state.

→ Support Others

Helping others is an evident path to personal growth. We often perceive "good individuals" as those who are willing to make sacrifices for others. This notion, in the minds of many, defines a person as "good." However, acts of kindness can also enhance our own well-being, as there is a strong link between selflessness and profound prosperity and happiness.

According to research, it is better to give than to receive. Therefore, even when you feel worried and busy, extending help to others, even when it's not necessary, can actually benefit you. By improving your ability to focus on the needs of others, you can experience personal growth.

So, yes, kindness is its reward and can help you alleviate stress. It concentrates on a show that selflessness is great for your close-to-home prosperity and can quantifiably upgrade your inner serenity.

One more concentrate on patients with Multiple Sclerosis (MS) showed that the individuals who offered other MS patients peer support experienced more prominent advantages than their upheld peers, including more articulated improvement of certainty, mindfulness, confidence, discouragement, and everyday working. The individuals who offered help commonly observed that their lives were emphatically different to improve things. Similarly, another study focusing on patients with Multiple Sclerosis (MS) revealed that those who offered peer support to fellow MS patients experienced greater benefits compared to those who received support. These benefits included improved confidence, mindfulness, self-esteem, reduced depression, and enhanced daily functioning. The individuals who provided support often reported that their own lives were positively transformed as a result.

In addition to making the world a better place, being selfless can also make you more compassionate and happier. The beauty of philanthropy lies in the fact that there are numerous ways to express it, making it an accessible path for anyone to become a better individual on a daily basis. This is certainly uplifting news.

→ *Influence Your Assets*

Forgetting about the time when caught up in an activity you love, commonly referred to as "flow" by psychologists, is a natural experience for many of us. Flow occurs when we become deeply immersed in a hobby, mastering a new skill or subject, or participating in activities that provide the perfect blend of challenge and ease.

At the point when we feel excessively tested, we feel anxious. At the point when things are excessively simple, we might become exhausted — one way or the other, figuring out the perfect balance between these two limits keeps us excellently taking part.

You can encounter flow by composing, moving, making, or by engrossing new material that you can instruct others. What might carry you to that condition might be trying for others and vice versa. Ponder when you end up in this state most frequently and take a stab at accomplishing more of that.

The condition of the flow is a decent sign of whether a movement is ideal for you. At the point when you're in a condition of stream, you're utilizing your assets, and this ends up being perfect for your profound well-being and joy

When you learn enough about yourself to understand your best assets and how to involve them in supporting others, you're en route to being a more joyful and superior individual.

→ *Utilize the "Phases of Progress" Model*

Ask yourself: If you had an enchanted wand, what might you want to find in your future? Disregarding the thoughts of how you'll arrive, distinctively envision your optimal life and what might be remembered for it.

Require a couple of moments to list, on paper or your PC, the progressions and objectives that would be remembered for this image. Be explicit about what you need Get it on paper.

You might follow the lead of numerous organizations and have a one-year, five-year, and 10-year plan for your life. (It doesn't need to be a firmly established plan, but a rundown of wishes and objectives.) Remembering what you expect in your future can assist you with feeling less trapped in the upsetting aspects of your current life and seeing more choices for change as they introduce themselves.

There are multiple ways of zeroing in on change, however, the phases of the progress model can lead you to the best version of yourself more effectively than in numerous different ways. This model of progress can be adjusted to anything you have at present and can work for the vast majority of new objectives.

The Phases of Progress Model

- Precontemplation: Disregarding the issue
- Thought: Mindful of the issue
- Readiness: Preparing to change
- Activity: Making an immediate move toward the objective
- Support: Keeping up with a new way of behaving
- Maintenance: Reaffirm your objective and obligation to change

One of the main pieces of this course to change is that you don't drive yourself to prepare changes before you're ready, and you don't surrender if you wind up breaking faith — it's an excusable and, surprisingly, anticipated piece of the course of progress. Understanding this arrangement for creating changes can assist you with being a superior individual in the ways you pick.

Deal with Yourself

EXTRACTING THE GOOD: THE IMPORTANCE OF SELF-LOVE

You may not necessarily have control over the conditions you face. Yet, you have some control over how well you deal with yourself, which can influence your anxiety and empower you to develop as an individual when facing life's difficulties.

Taking care of oneself is fundamental for building strength while confronting undeniable stressors for a few reasons. When you're drained, eating ineffectively, or by and large neglected, you will be more receptive to the pressure you face in your life. You might make more issues for yourself by responding inadequately instead of answering from a quiet, inward-strength position.

On the other hand, while you're taking great consideration of yourself (both your body and mind), you can be all the more mindfully drawn in with anything that comes, utilize the assets you have in your life, and develop from the difficulties you face, as opposed to simply enduring them.

Taking legitimate consideration of your life elements can save you and keep you in ideal shape for dealing with pressure. This gives you added strength to deal with your life difficulties and those that might be valued to you.

Importance of Taking Care of Yourself

As far as taking care of oneself techniques, there are a few that can help, yet probably the main parts of taking care of oneself incorporate the essentials:

Rest

Rest is significant for your profound and actual prosperity because too little or low-quality rest can leave you feeling more worried and less ready to conceptualize answers to issues you face. Absence of rest can negatively affect your body, too, for the time being, and over the long haul. Unfortunately, rest might influence your weight.

Sustenance

A less-than-stellar eating routine can leave you feeling swollen and tired and can add additional pounds after some time. You want the right fuel to confront life's difficulties; however, when stress hits, it's not unexpected the undesirable food we pine for.

Social Associations

Feeling associated with others can assist you with feeling stronger. Old buddies can assist you with handling gloomy feelings, conceptualizing arrangements, and getting your brain off your concerns when important. It's occasionally difficult to carve out an opportunity for companions when you have an occupied, distressing life; however, our companions frequently improve us individuals with their help and motivation.

Free time

At long last, reserving a little margin for yourself is significant. This can mean journaling and contemplation, or it can come as exercise or, in any event, watching reruns at home. This is especially significant for contemplative people, yet everybody needs an opportunity to themselves occasionally.

Figure out how to Be Easy to use

Our relationships can help us shelter from pressure and assist us with turning out to be better individuals simultaneously. They can likewise be a critical wellspring of stress when a struggle is settled inadequately or passed on to deteriorate. The excellence of this is that as we accomplish the work it takes to improve as a companion, friend, and relative, it can likewise be a way to improve personally.

To work on your connections and yourself, learn

compromise methodologies. These incorporate being a decent audience and understanding the opposite side when you struggle.

These things can assist us with being better variants of ourselves. They can likewise limit the pressure we experience in connections and make us more grounded. Also, cozy connections give you many chances to rehearse these abilities as you further develop them, so you can try and value the open doors when they emerge and feel less steamed.

CONCLUSION

Everything we have discussed so far is to help you become the best version of yourself. Everybody needs to turn into their best selves, but only a few make it happen. You've finally chosen to chip away at the best version of yourself; however, what does that term mean?

The meaning of "best self" is emotional. Your style of being the best version of yourself may not be equivalent to your family or friends. Considering this, don't give in to the pressure of comparing yourself to others. Define your best version of yourself for yourself.

Also, your "best self" should be open to improvements; it doesn't have to be the same forever. After some time, your meaning of the best version of yourself will change in all aspects of your life, so make it a point to be adaptable.

For some others, the best version of yourself involves taking control of your life. When you make a choice, you become more determined to pursue it to your satisfaction.

More than that, being the best version of yourself doesn't mean winning 100% all of the time. All aspects of your life can't turn out how you want it to at the same time. Life doesn't work that way. Instead, being the best version of yourself is your ability to face life's tests and confront challenges head-on.

Regardless of what you may try to find out, you'll stop at the realization that being the best version of yourself is not a short-term goal. Sometimes, it can take a lifetime. So, gird yourself for the ride, and enjoy the journey.

May you extract the good from life and always leave room for self-love.

-Alberta Lampkins

NOTES TO SELF

love yourself. ♥

READING GROUP DISCUSSION QUESTIONS AND ACTIVITY

1. What makes you unique?

2. What makes you feel good about yourself?

3. What does the word "self-love" mean to you? What are three examples of self-love?

4. What things do you do for self-care?

5. How could you simplify your life and focus on what is most important?

Ask the group to create a list of self-love affirmations and encourage them to be creative. Hopefully, everyone will leave with positive words of inspiration, positivity, and encouragement. Be unique. Be You!

Great News!

When Alberta began working on her book, *Extracting the Good: The Importance of Self-Love,* each chapter served as a source of strength and guidance for her life's journey. She discovered how divine self-love is and the importance of being the best version of yourself. Her book moved her, so, she turned it into a workshop, and she wants to impart the discovery of gratitude and how to embrace self-love with YOU.

Workshop Title: Embracing You: A Journey to Discovery and Cultivating Self-Love

In this 3.5-hour self-discovery workshop, you will:

- Explore what makes you unique.
- Understand the importance of embracing your uniqueness.
- Know the concept and importance of self-love.
- Explore strategies for managing self-care.
- Develop an action plan for personal growth based on the "Stages of Change" Model.
- Apply the learned concepts to your life.

What your admission fee gets you?

- Appetizing brunch food and drinks.
- Hands-on self-love exercises, tips, and techniques.
- Interactive Self-Love Workbook
- Self-care goody bag.
- An amazing experience!

Book this workshop for your next Event!
www.albertalampkins.com
albertalampkins@gmail.com

ABOUT THE AUTHOR

Alberta Lampkins is an author, educator, motivator, mentor, and community leader. She is the Affiliate Director of a youth mentoring program and an Adjunct Sociology Professor at Fayetteville State University.

Alberta is also the founder and publisher of A.L. Savvy Publications, an independent self-publishing company she created in 2014.

Alberta is the author of *Teach Me How to Fly* and visionary of *Messages to Our Children* and *Speak Young Brown People, Speak. We are Listening*.

Alberta holds a Master of Arts in Sociology from Fayetteville State University. Her graduate research project on HIV testing among African-American women was proudly accepted for scholarly publication in the *Journal of Research on Women and Gender*, Texas State University.

Alberta is also a member of Zeta Phi Beta Sorority, Inc.

Alberta is married to Command Sergeant Major Al Lampkins (Retired U.S. Army). Together, they have two amazing adult children, Alexis and Ahmad, and one very handsome grandson, Elijah. Their family is soon to grow.

Alberta Lampkins is a native of Buffalo, New York. However, she resides in North Carolina with her family.

www.ingramcontent.com/pod-product-compliance
Lightning Source LLC
Chambersburg PA
CBHW070737020526
44118CB00035B/1414